THE ESSENCE

By:
Miranda Baron

Dedication

To You: The one who has figured yourself out so deeply,
that all you have to do is "Be You" completely.

About the Author

Miranda Baron

As someone who enjoys romanticizing a simple life, Miranda is an artist among many mediums. When she's not grooming dogs or writing in her spare time, you can expect her to be playing piano, crocheting hats and blankets, wood burning, painting, hiking and enjoying a nice walk in the park. With her two cats, friends and family, this author has found happiness enjoying a slow paced life of love, animals, and comfortability.

Contents

"I've tried to reduce profanity but I reduced so much profanity when writing the book that I'm afraid not much could come out. Perhaps we will have to consider it simply as a profane book and hope that the next book will be less profane or perhaps more sacred."

-Ernest Hemingway

I looked in the mirror,
Smiled and said
"Welcome Back!"
M.B.

24 Ways
(To keep me in place)
Enveloped by C.S.F.
(with each vertebrae)
Synapses and receptors alike
(shaping the body with a spine)
each notion of motion
(guided by figments of emotion)
with a form of connection so bizarre.
(energies and intuition align)
Here be a brain, understanding itself
(everlasting and everchanging, awareness in the mind)
with philosophies shared over time.
(all becoming- a collective energy)
Truth, Love, Understanding
(and <u>mind</u>, <u>matter</u>, <u>energy</u> combined)

THE ESSENCE

A Note From the Author

Abundance. A word defined as the plentifulness of good things in life and living with prosperity. For many, this word is the epitome of receiving a surplus of all that glitters and calling it gold. However, many people seem to struggle with the truth of what abundance is and how to attain, obtain and maintain such a lifestyle within their version of reality. I'm not here to bore, lecture or enlighten you on the tens of thousands of ways to align your mind to get what you want over time; if you so choose, that will be your mission. A simple purpose of this life is to be able to create happiness within, knowing you are not alone, and love. You see, until your subconscious believes in the infinite possibilities of our metaphysical existence, no amount of redundant explanations nor scriptures memorized verbatim will shift your paradigm to live with glory and prosperity like it's the movies. One must want to live independently without the fantasy and preconceived notion that glory is vicariously relishing in the image of the prosperity of another's life. Living with a higher *vibration* within this time-continuum vortex and practicing a lifestyle abiding by the Laws of Attraction and principles of what is and always has been is all a part of the higher message I'd love to relay, but that is a choice within the mind you must make. Like you, I am just another somebody in this world of over 7 billion who is trying to understand why we live upon this land and appreciate a world where we all can live the life of our dreams and have that "fairytale happy ending."

With all the trials and tribulations we endure along this passing lifetime, sometimes the best of us seem to fall apart, lose the sense of ourselves, our family and loved ones, and find that "knight in shining armor" we've been waiting for, seems to have fallen off his trusty steed and got lost in the fog of the forest somewhere along the way. Many ask how we deal with the lonely, sleepless nights without that special somebody by our side?

Well, we do what every other person in history, young or old, does in that situation- deal with it. When you learn to pave a path of your own, you'll start to build a love for yourself, and each day, when you look in the mirror, you will remember who you truly are meant to be. You will be thankful for the alone time and realize the simple beauty of being oneself. Listen to the inner voice guiding you to recreate and realign yourself with the life you want, this message is a gift meant just for you. Don't be fooled; there will always be some form of positivity and negativity that will help you balance your shift in many ways. The reality of which you bring will be that of which thought process you choose. There is strength in the ability to create something greater than yourself, and this begins with the lifestyle you abide by. Enable yourself to live for something new; look forward to the break of dawn, the sunrise and morning walks, casual encounters and pep talks; allow yourself to cherish the day regardless of your physical state. Whether you are physically incapable, a stay-at-home individual, someone who can work on the go, or always somewhere new on a roll- the reality you create over time begins with your state of mind, so think wisely.

When you spend time alone, or with friends and family you so dearly hold close, you will figure out what your ego wants and what you need to nourish your mind-body and soul. Abundance can hit you with more than you have ever felt, leaving you dealing with cards you've never held. I want you to find the strength to be love anyway, embrace your passion and fight to heal through your pain. This will be tricky to read between the lines, learn from the hidden messages, and follow the rules to help you play the game. Once you do, define your name!

Find your inner strength and figure out a way to encourage yourself to accept the gift of the momentary presence of each day. Through the *good* times and *bad*, seek for what you want- not what you've had. Find the *balance* that allows you to separate one thing from another; know there is beauty in a new beginning in life even after the regression of which *consequences* we had to suffer. Acknowledge the natural *ebb and flow,* and when you feel like you're holding on too tight- remember to let it go.

The time it takes for you to act upon thought and idea means there is already energy allowing that reality to come to fruition. That new life you seek is already manifesting at a new beginning, as it has formed *within,* and once spoken *out,* you have given that thought and idea the power to transform and grow. Everything is *energy*, and the sooner we accept that the sooner our reality will *correspond* with all that. We (as more than just physical beings) will be motivated to live for a greater purpose. Once we begin along this path, there is no going back. Awareness of *All*- that of which we are, enables us to transform. This delicate and intricate way of thinking will take you out of your paradigm of normality and structure to conform and grant you the power to live being something and someone more.

Abundance is everything you've been granted, nothing less, and this life of which we live is our test. There will be moments in life when we are faced with truth. What will we do with it? There will be people who are so helplessly yearning for love. Will we have the strength to create healthy boundaries and open up? There will be situations that happen beyond our control.

Will we accept all that we do and do not know? We must understand that there is so much more than 'sunshine and golden rainbows' or 'mercury rivers and enchantment' upon our imaginative golden land. There is a reality greater than just me and you. Reality is shifting with every fleeting moment of the present, and each moment of time is a gift if we choose to live with awareness. When we practice living within our *truths*, being open for *love* and *understanding* the larger picture, we will begin to know ourselves more and exist as more than just our thoughts, memories and the figments of our imagination.

Every individual has the capacity to recreate their reality, change their self-image and live with intention. Every bit of who we are mentally, physically and spiritually can be shifted and created into the version of ourselves we seek to be. We must confront our 'self' and break through the doubt and illusions that hold us back. Abundance is every bit of this; it can be one's greatest gift when harnessed correctly.

The essence of our being is something greater than what we are used to perceiving. Reality is defined as the state of being as it exists, and our paradigm, through that concept, can shift. As you read the forthcoming writings, I'd like you to understand that there is much truth in my messages.

Many of the alliterations and characterizations I have created mirror a form of truth through perception. We are a very intricate and complex species that lives in a time of revelations, technological advancements and industrialization. There are many things of which we experience and see that come to us with uncertainty. This has been pushing me to understand beyond the emotional self and ego of 'me'.

Since THE ELEMENTS have been exposed, I have been confronted by the connection of individuals' paths and truths of what so many of us are affected by and go through. It is with my greatest regard that the willpower of every individual reading my words can and will have the strength to identify a situation and make the right decision going forward to create a better life for themselves.

You will know you have made the right decision when your mind is clear and you have peace inside. I hereby expose you to the essence of all connected beings, the all-seeing and all-believing greatness within, and express it with a poetic twist. Many excerpts have been altered, and situations have been personified in various contexts to relay a deeper message of the inevitable truths, unconditional love, and understanding variations.

With love and sincerity,

Miranda Baron

M.B.

TRUTH

ILLUSION

Afraid of the Dark

You weren't afraid of the dark
you were afraid of the voices in your head,
the cracked door that slams in the wind- BOOM!
Have you found any monsters under the bed?
How about an extra shadow in your room?
What's the lack of photons
when there's nothing but silence in your mind that goes on?
Accept who you are
and set fire with a spark
blinding the barriers of your room
photosynthesizing a new self in bloom.
You were never afraid of the dark,
you were just afraid of you.
Once you've made the day from night,
it's time to really live your life.

AnyWayThruToday

When your heart stops relating,
your mind starts debating,
contradicting what you're saying.

With one finger on the trigger
and the other three staring at me,
loss be of thy hands quivering,
striving for redamancy,
cutting cords- forgiving,
leaving all that's left of me.

Hushing me with my big words
and gifts you see,
here be a virago of a woman
only showing you
what I want you to believe.
Self-evaluation
drowning in self-pity-
they want reflection
(but with the smoke in the mirrors)
I can barely see
let alone believe
the lies I've lived
that were greater than me.
It's all meant as fun and games
and then came year 18
"it's just what happens,
sometimes love doesn't stay."
but I wasn't aware then, that
he was the second man to that day;
they both walked away.
And I'm not the same.
I wrote a new chapter,
turned the page,
lived with a new family,
as my mother was locked, caged, then set free-
to start a sober life, showing strength and equality.

Now its' just the truth and me,
the only other plot twist since "Year 23"
was that I did whatever it takes-
to make it in this life, I won't break.
Messages to myself so the memories
never die in vein
"I still love you, anyway".

A new verse scripted on a lined page
with lines of minds lost in the same wave-
when people ask me what made me this way,
when I nod and feel the pain in their poetry,
when they are screaming loud to the back of the crowd,
I just smile and say, "I can relate."
we've all got a story to share
but we've got to live thru the pain
never speak in vein,
have faith, don't go insane,
Just smile when you say
"Love, anyways."

Big Bad Wolf

She drank from his chalice
a bittersweet aftertaste
a remembrance
transcending into existence.

They call it healing
lost in the trance
meditation-
at a glance;
this tonic
the wicked man's brew,
sweet chocolate
to help you through
the tears to come.
Hypnotized
you stay in your place
submitting, in the darkness you lay
to the one domineering
making you the weak one, sneering.

This renaissance, each seance
was a trap lead to
the one who could rescue, protect,
expose, and victimize you, discrete
with his shamanic ways- his
narcissistic toxicity creates those wicked games to play.

Rapunzel can't let her hair down,
Snow won't wake from her sleep,
Cinderella ran out of time and
Belle lives stuck with this Beast.

Drink from the chalice
as you may
the big dogs bite less
their barks are all play;
and they'll bitch
and they'll moan

with their huffing and puffing
and leaving you alone-
let alone, without a heart to hold.

Paper thin and
gone with the wind, this man
is at it again.
Silence in town
women in dismay
something's gone wrong
this isn't the healing way.
A selfish game
sick seduction, he played.
Little Red won't get lost
dead in the woods, she'll never lay
never again on such land,
never again, for such a man.

"Hey, Big Bad Wolf.
Here I Am.
I've got your chalice
and I'm in a jam.
Let me tell you about this mess,
let me tell you, I just can't bear to stand-"
hands over chalice
"unless it's to the man
who took this chalice from my hand
to show it's a safe sip, and say-"

"I'm the only man..."
Stopped in his tracks-
choking on revenge
the potion was not a cure
instead, a poison, he's sure,
flows within him to this day.
"You may have been the Big Bad Wolf, but my house is made of bricks, bitch.
Fooled me once, but I won't fall for this trick.
You're going to just huff and puff and blow, again."

Bright Light

This is how you kill a demon
when the monster looks you in the eyes:
Fight with light
and summon the angels in your life.
You can be all of who you are
radiating positivity ranging near and far.
Light up the world
of which you're upon
because demons live in the lives
of those who think all hope is gone.

BrokenChain

Perhaps, maybe
they're just seeing it all wrong.
Perhaps, maybe
they've got their beer goggles on.
Perhaps, maybe
it's just another broken record
trying to play a song,
trying to get along,
trying to write a line and
leaving out the lost love.
It's gone.
Gone in the wind,
lost in the sins,
gone with the good words
and all that could have been.
Perhaps, maybe
they're reading it all wrong
Perhaps, maybe
they relate all along.
Perhaps, maybe
it was a lie too strong,
trying to hold on,
dying to get along
living just to hold on.
Hoping and praying
Disillusion, front and center stage
remembering the old ways
calling the old names
wishing for the same thing
missing a link for a broken chain.
A broken chain, linked by pain
break the shackles,
start a new day.
Nothing will be the same
it's nothing, just bottled pain,
it's nothing but insane,
trying to mend something
that was broken since the first day

Cloud tear

One would think
The ocean had drowned in enough of the clouds' tears.
Yet here I sit, feeding it more,
with only screams left to hear.

Cookie Cutter Scriptures

Another cookie cutter
another basic someone-or another,
just don't be of blame
when they're all just the same-
poetry of sadness, ripples to wade
A smile and a wave,
you must be insane.
Illiterate words from other books
vernacular disheveled, you're left shook.
Another 15 and the cookies nearly burnt
that's a lesson maybe you'll learn.

A delicate, raw, sweet to the taste
enters the oven, preparing to bake.
But what happens when the chef walks away
, dishing out to serve another plate?
Trapped in a sauna
all you 'oughta do
is let it burn,
forgot to flip,
no room to turn.
Words fill the chocolate drain
a trail of chocolate death along the tray.

Another 2 minutes, and the chef comes to play
, cooling and drooling, for these savages they prey.
Dipped in a glacier, prepped, feel the breathing
a simple bite, and for the All, you'd fight.

But you're just a little cookie,
and those are just a little chocolate-drizzled words,
turn the tables
listen to my stories you call fables,
pour the milk, dish it and serve.
Did you think you knew me?
Just by the way, I've let you learn?

Even if you're raw, even if you're burned-
Leave it to the cookie cutters,
to decorate the platters,
but leave it to the TLC, a secret ingredient of honey
found on the open road,
a sweet treat was saved special to not compete.
Another dozen has been turned,
flipped and served,
delivered in a package signed for the world
labeled for all to see:
"Enjoy, fresh baked cookies!"

Another batch just the same,
I leave you
in ways of words, some've never heard
with cookies on your brain.

Cryin' Wolf

Judge me as you want
it is not what you thought
I gave you my trust
but the front door was locked.
So I yearned, and I learned
to speak in your tongue
I gave you my truth
I thought you'd open up.

But now it's my book
that's opened up to the page,
unwritten: YOUR NAME,
You thought I was a Fake!?
A facade in your face
mistaken my youth with ignorance
go ahead- tell it to my face
how you think I'm naïeve yet
when I close my eyes
and travel beyond the skies
aligning my energies
with rapid movement
behind shut eyes
you think what you can't see is lies?
History, a tale as old as time,
we are all unique! We are all divine!

Yet I'm the one who's untrue
when I've never once said a bad thing about you?

So, tell it to my face when my mind wanders
to that dark place, and there's no-one around
to pick me up when I'm down.
All I do is scream, yet no one hears a sound
Cryin' Wolf as I'm pinned to the ground.
Maybe one day you'll listen to me,
and then you'll know
when I'm speaking to you
from ten feet below.

DarKnight

You held the shadows
where my sadness chose to lay.
You were the empty train track
accompanied by fog-
not the passengers
heading out
for a journey that day,
giving me space.
You were the hope in a family photograph
saved after the house burnt down.
You were the only phone call
when no-one else
was around.

You were the darkness
where the shadows chose to lay
you were the last train
to depart with one passenger that day.

She cried, "My foreboden filled heart,
"Oh, how it didn't love enough", as he would claim.
Have I let my mind get in my heart's way?"
But he loved her endlessly, anyway.

You were the old photographs
where everything appeared alright.
The light in the darkness
signaling my way.
But you are no longer
the person I call at night.
Now, my strength and faith
have accompanied me the same,
just in time- letting me know it's because of light
a little darkness is alright.

Deceptive

This world is a game full of
miracles and blessings,
lies and deception.
If anyone tries to tell you any different
that's just their perspective.

Destiny Remedy

There was a time
where within the mind
all we felt, was pure sublime.

And we'd wine
then we'd dine
making great with those who
pass our way, never counting
how long they'd stay,
it's just another blessing,
just another reason to pray.

Now we believe
that all is meant to happen
because all that is- shall be-
just another piece
of a puzzle we call Destiny.

Doubledhistake

Rollercoaster was an understatement-
under the statements she made.

"Hold that tongue, or it's mine to take!"
Another empty bottle,
another quick flick,
another moan and groan,
another thrust,
another shake,
another hit,
another break
aimed 'fore the queue, striked out
lights out, last call, it's a black ball
bending and spending
until the next day;
poisoning your tonic
he's stiff as you lay-
alone, in his bed
alone, in your head
you sit, as she bends.
Her back bends, meanwhile
on his next bend
he's at it again-
another ruthless vulture
another has been
another "Fuck you, it's over"
alone, you sit sober,
alone, he wants you closer,
alone, it feels over,
alone, time feels slower
passing time, another line
another bar bump and grind.
Heat it up and take another line
<WAKE UP!!>
It's no longer party time.
Red (white) and blue
stay true to you- with his
deceit on the scene

nobody left to be seen
he's all black and blue-
no-body to come thru
nobody would want to.
Have you some-body to run to?
Somebody is your favorite tune-
that rings as your tears sting-
don't answer the phone,
it's not meant to be you;
You Are Worth More Than He Has Put You Through.

Draw

The truth cuts like a siv
releasing pressure
from the outside,
a fresh way to
oxidize what is trapped within-
darkness craves
for you to give in.
Pulling you by your misery,
subliminally.
Can't you see?
You cannot keep the darkness within,
if it surfaces like a malicious sin,
your loss will be your demon's greatest win.

Duplicity is toxicity.
Draw out your pain
like toxic lead
forced upon paper so plain-
every line, your next lead
so thin(k) once again, you gain-
the ability to recreate,
shine a light on your darkness
as you sketch upon every page.
Replacing that rage,
an illustrated token
of words unspoken,
a fragment of you
upon this page;
a beacon of hope to help let go
and change your ways
on the darkest of days.
Draw out the pain.
Recreate.

Family Dreams

This world is no place for the weak
another habit forms an addict
selfish, to rely on the stitch that holds the seams;
alone, so it seems, failing the legacy of family dreams.

This world is no place for the weak
another has been, looking towards 'back when'
tossing and turning, just taking another for the team,
alone, so it seems, failing the legacy of family dreams.

This world is no place for the weak
crippling at the knees, losing the light that sparks,
mind lost in the dark, stuck in bed- mad in the head,
alone, so it seems, failing the legacy of family dreams.

This world is no place for the weak
another walk along the streets
helpless to the way things could be
alone, so it seems, failing the legacy of family dreams.

This world is no place for the weak
another toke to crack a joke
losing faith in humanity, lost within insanity
alone, so it seems, failing the legacy of family dreams.

This world is no place for the weak
thriving to replace the fear of dying
crippling remorse, faith in a higher source,
alone, so it seems, failing the legacy of family dreams.

This world is no place for the weak
another conspiracy to believe
lost in time, when nothing feels right
alone, so it seems, failing the legacy of family dreams.

This world is no place for the weak
another victim, the captor creates the schism
locked into a life where disillusion reaps,

alone, so it seems, failing the legacy of family dreams.

This world is no place for the weak
another turns cold, casting figments into stone,
alone, so it seems, failing the legacy of family dreams.

This world is no place for the weak
building a better life to replace the disgrace
all it takes is every bit of strength to not feel-
alone- so it seems, failing the legacy of family dreams.

Fairly BlasTheMe

Another page
to purge the pain.
Clock strikes midnight
and all her beauty
went away.

A house of glass
how fragile is that?
Another "To Be"
another slap of reality-
awakened from her
fairly tail tall-tell blasphemy
with an ego that never let
truth be as equal.

What's the matter of a *mind*
with a broken heart
barely mending over *time*?

Another smoke,
a sip of wine,
another hurtful trend
replaying like the last time.
With the thought of a shot
of Mother's Medicine, going on and on
killing the memories just to mend.

Fairytale Badlands

You were the greatest love story
that never played out
arrythmia of my heart
skipping your way-
uniting with happiness
after being led too far astray
our bodies connected
our minds on the same wave.
We never Pan'd out.
We never flew away.

And neverland, I'll never land, and
never will a man
take my hand
with broken promises
and a predator's way
to possess and lead sanity as prey
illusion and madness stray to another land.
Oh, wonderland,
wonder when'll be the day
no fool lost the way
and no caterpillar every packed a pipe and didn't stay
where no cat cloaks in the light today
and no man could ever drop the hand
of an Alice that just happened to matter to the Hatter.

F1

One person's fiction
lives in another person's facts.
Don't believe the truth?
Here's some shoes,
why don't you take a walk back-
into their past
to see that which is only a story to you,
has been a reality come true.
Cinderella never found her glass slipper,
her Prince Charming never came through-
as her evil stepsisters held back all they ever knew
for a piece of her glory,
when her moment, her story,
became something new.

F2

New to me
could be old to you,
what's chaos for me
could be normal to the next boy in blue.
Walk softly upon a golden forest
shimmering within the mercury rivers,
fear not, my oasis
those are just shivers we can see,
warn me when you get the quivers-
that's when we feel what's unseen.

Is my reality a little different?
Each poem a puzzle of blatant scenes?
Imagination so vivid
when my reality is living
within the abyss of a mind, filled with
golden forests greater than we've ever dreamed.

Lonely Attacks

There's blood in the shower
because she's been crying for hours.
She hates feeling this way.
These lonely attacks feel like
they never go too far astray.

Mirror Mirror

There's a difference
between unraveling at the seams
like stitches upon the skin,
and throwing a boulder
at a glass mirror
after it says
"nothing is fair, after all."

Oh, mirror mirror on the wall
When will it be my turn to be the fairest-
of the All, you speak, telling me how I should be,
telling me what you see, is just your version of reality,
telling me all is fair to sow that which we reap.
And mirror, oh mirror, when shall be the day
a glass slipper and a gift to kiss her will be come what may-
for this absent mind and heart that cries for a Prince to stay,
so charming, yet alarming how you've not shown me the way.
Mirror mirror on the wall: what are these games you play?

MirrorMan

You broke through my armor
as though
I hadn't just spent
the past 8 years, carefully
designing every meticulous piece-
protecting the heart on my sleeve,
protecting a mind that thinks-
hope is the key to believe.
You broke me through my armor
you broke through to me,
without hesitating-
head-first, initiating, breaking-
as though I was wearing
some nickel worthy coke can armor,
with a mind as fragile as a half-damp
paper plate, you thought you could just disarm-
that whole image of who you thought I am.
Yet here I stand, strong on my own
heart of gold ready for the thrown;
as a jester, you speak,
with my mirror in hand,
I give my last damn.

Get out of my Kingdom, man.

The Music

They say they love the music
because that was the only thing around
when their friends threw up the deuces
and left them clueless;
but it wasn't the music
it was never the music
it was the way they were feeling
when they decided what to do with it.

New Boundary

It's a love story,
fairytale cloaked as glory,
fiction fantasy, poem or prose,
it's a short story.

When It's all over.
If you're writing about it
you've moved on.
Move on, for so long and
so on, until it's gone.
Then, start writing
your new story.
Illuminate the mercury rivers
with the sun's golden glory.
Step into your new reality.
Let go of every catastrophe
it was all blasphemy.
Bring forth all the love,
healing, happiness, and empathy,
beauty lives in every word worth writing:
the greatest battle of one's own heart and mind
is worth fighting.
Harness the greatness of everything
new that is happening that's your power.
Be yourself completely, never walk discreetly
even after the clock strikes upon the new hour.

Old News-New to You

I could be in the middle of the limelight
while the time right
with my rhymes tight
and my future in clear sight;
but nothing compares to those late nights
when all I want is something new.
But I'm sitting here starting to feel blue
they sayin' "I'mma come thru"
but all I have to do
is sit around and watch you do you
because for me, that's all old news.
And I see people like me
for what it is that I can do.
It's not luck, man!
It's what I had to!
This is just a part of me
just the character I had to be
when there was nobody around for real soul food.
You think my art is beautiful
but what about the loneliness I had to go through?

They tell me not to trust
but question why I've got trust issues.

There was just a couple things I had to learn,
bout the lessons of love and the way people are misused,
and now that's made me that person you look up to.

So next time you hit me up to come thru
just know I'mma do me
'cus I'm not a damn fool-
fool me once
I might be the one you can run to
fool me twice
why you trickin' me to run with you
fool me three times, fuck-you get the peace sign
now it's pay the price time
step back, I'm on the front line

you've a quarter-back?
I've got a quarter bag
smoked yours and all mine.
Think you've got depth?
I'm swimming in high tide,
High on life, writing to keep
My mind right-
here is where I need to be
disillusioned- this illusion
is far from what I used to see.
The tortoise and the hare
will finish the race eventually
it's either them or me
placed on the front line,
it's crunch time,
are you where you need to be?
You're way back, and I'm up-
hunting like a wild cat,
where's your mind at?
Like a hi-hat
speaks the beat in cut time-
there's my punchline,
words served like it's lunch time
go find a place to eat the words that feel safe.

I've finished the race,
while you're still running in place.

PageTurned

There was a dope dealer
on every corner
another slow healer
chemical imbalance disorder
another small town
zooming in, lens on the Benz
the time is getting closer;
slow drag and a sip a little slower
someone made a slow turn,
left on the streets;
in the right lane, gears changed
move over, don't freak out- of their mind,
a tweakin' fiend slaps the hands with something unseen,
life's cut pays a little lower, another buck from his fellow stoner.

This is more than I can bear to see.
I've got to leave,
hit the highway at full speed
next town over
palm trees, salty summer breeze
find me where my poverty is relieved
as I switch gears, my vision of my own life clear
living the life I've earned, a new beginning is near.

Full platter with a cake well served
a change of mind changed the way my world turned,
living by my own terms, and accepting the new life I deserve.

Q♥

Maybe it was the queen
the pinnacle of difficulty
that kept pushing them away
and cried for them to stay.

Maybe it was me
falsifying the reality
that must be why they think I'm fake
yet I live a life they'd love to take.

Maybe it was the queen
who cried the loudest scream
when everyone went astray
and felt alone that day.

Maybe it was me
that lead them to believe
I had something more to say
but chose not to trust, either way-

Now their heart is a marionette
for the queen to play.

#replaced

So out of place
how can I escape?
Lost in a holographic pixelated maze-
electromagnetic radio waves,
toxic plasticity within their brains
losing loved ones to the insane
prescribed pills to lose the thrill,
another deranged face gets a "like" hooray!
Mirrored pixels rearranged
doe eyes and lust to close the day.
Society's latest taboo,
what does it matter to people like me and you?
The unaware have no clue
they're too late for saving grace.
Check their latest selfie, lost within themselves, see
a hashtag. Replaced.

Spoon of Lie Pie

Marionette.
Like a puppet
without a mind;
just a mime
that can't say
what's on my mind,
because all I am
is your puppet
rewriting your story
in the present
with my time
in my life.

I was blind
and disguised
spoon-fed the best
taste of lies,
now I lie
in my bed
and try to decide
what's going on in my head
I've blindfolded my mind's eye,
listening to my thoughts,
am I better off-
Dead or alive?
Investing my life with
the last thing I bought
was the ability to copywrite.
They can't copy me-right?
All I ever thought
is now a battle in my mind
just another way to pass the time.
I'll be alright
This is what I do when I fall asleep at night.

Tis T'Eve

Those nights always felt like Christmas Eve-
back when you were a child
and the adrenaline drove you wild
in anticipation, just waiting
for that moment, you awaken.
Reality shifted, realizing you've been gifted
with something new-
meant just for you;
another blessin' another lesson
another childhood dream come true.

Those nights, I had the most peace
ironic, that's when I couldn't fall asleep
funny, that's when I can't control if I laugh or scream.
All I want is to believe; all I want is to finally see-
the gift of the presence, awareness-
that simple, timeless moment of bliss;
when all I feel is
A New Reason To Live.

Like a dream come true
all I want to do
all I want to do
like a dream come true
all I want to do
all I want to do
is be present with you.

Tr.E.N.D.

He wonders why I'm hard to love.

(When love chose drugs
she left me alone as one
it's simple subtraction
as division corrupts.

Struck-
right in the heart
again, again, again,
until we were literally forced apart.

Physically, she was given a new heart
for a new life to start.
Mentally, it turned to art,
living a life looking for light
choosing to stay in the dark).

And there, you are;
I've come so far.

He's just another some-one or another
striving for a happy ending slumber.
Penny for the pepper-spray to make him stay.
He paid the price; I'm smarter than they say.

When they claim I hurt them, I remember the pain
learning, from actions to this day.
Can I predict the habits of a trend?
Roll the dice?
Poker Face for the men.
An educated guess says they'll fuck up what comes next!
Must you play your cards right?
Overcompensating, Red flags in sight.

Everyone wants to see me. Oh, so nice!
But that's not always real life.

Another lesson-
tempers' testin'
lies right to my eyes
disguised over time,
but these blue eyes ain't blind;
and in time, I find:

One cannot deceit me
when there is nothing in this world
that I *feel* bleakly.

25 and Free for Life

Some will call it insanity
confronting one's own darkness
an alliance of calamity
perplexed with emotion
a mind-warped distortion
is blasphemy, succumbing
to the shadows, what's happening?

It's saddening
call the doctor, call the family.
Haven't learned the lesson,
internal demons battling'.
For what? The troubles built up
like pouring concrete into a glass cup,
then you act up when the meds' stacked' up.
<u>Truth</u> is a hard pill to swallow
a knife to the chest,
loaded barrel-
kills the sorrows
when the heart feels hollow,
mind lost in yesterday,
losing hope for tomorrow.

Now, the pew prays.
Who's to save Grace?
Thirty seconds left
until her next hurricane,
a dose of "Mother's Medicine."
to kill the pain.
Life is God's gift,
yet negative energy
to positivity is a change.
Chemical imbalance
flooding the brain;
one more thought
and nothing's ever
going to be the same.

Learn from another's lesson,
change the game.
Speak Truth to Fight Depression.
Figments of reality
keep calling a name,
but the energy never dies,
so stop with the selfish ways.

A victim in digression
creating one's own depression
Fight or flight; it's a bad day-
not a bad life. Memories fade away
no cycle of remembering and regretting
will ever make things right.

One must take control
of their own life. A balance,
the strife, and when yin
swam in her darkness-
she was blessed with yang's
duality of light.

There's a way of finding
eloquence within THE ELEMENTS
of every individual's life;
a ribbon of hope strung tight
to help all find the light.
Another verse is beneath the surface
giving Faith a new form of life;
living like Love: So patient, so Kind.
Climbing the stairway to Heaven
like everything, it will take time.
Just make yourself a promise
to always do what is right.

Time Travel

Back to the future
of a reality none the same
of holographic materials
and resonating energy waves.

Back to the past
in a world uninhabited
with vines suffocating lives
and historic bodies decayed.

Back to the present
within this moment you live;
awareness- the gift
your essence is to embrace.

Upon the Golden Land

She knew exactly what she was up against
sword in hand
armor abroad skin
mind in a golden forest
where no imposer worth letting in.
And deeper and deeper she goes
into that forest, unknown,
fighting demons on the land of her very own
kingdom she calls home.

She knew exactly what she was up against
sword in hand
armor abroad skin
mind in a golden forest
treading mercury rivers
following Alice and Peter
to where the lost boys like to go.

She knew exactly what she was up against
sword in hand
armor abroad skin
mind in a golden forest
calling from the bottom of the rabbit hole,
again, falling, again, and again, and then
-because forbid it to be actual chivalry of real men,
she took the hand of the ever-young Pan
flying to where only he and she can-
make tendencies, turn to memories,
waking alone in the forest
again and again.
Blasphemy! She cries against more men.

She knew exactly what she was up against
sword in hand
armor abroad skin
mind in a golden forest
heart in the queen's hand.
One foul breath and that's all that's to be left,

of an armored girl-trapped in the hands of another,
among her own land.

She knew exactly what she was up against
sword in hand
mind in a golden forest
no more, no such galore.
A figment of reality to believe
and believe that which is not seen.

Armor on the floor,
another vile taken to make her think
reality changes in just a blink.
She knew exactly what she was up against
an old-fashioned dreamer
in the modern conformed day and age.
Forced to stop believing
unless it's to their one all mighty that you pray.

Armored no more, as raw as she could be,
pills in the poison bowl, mind in a rabbit hole.
Never let anyone claim her crazed
as she freed herself from the shackles of the modern age.

She knew exactly what she was up against
sword in hand
armor abroad skin
mind in a golden forest
mercury rivers flowing within.
Demons only stay until she slays,
reclaiming a kingdom of her own to peacefully live in.

She knew exactly what she was up against
sword in hand
armor no longer upon her skin
mind in a golden forest
baths in pure rivers, cleansing sins
in rays and figments of light guiding her to
another land other than a wonderland where no one could
ever stand in her way.

Vines

Nobody warns the tree's
that the leaves will begin to change
there's no head's up on how
they'll evolve
from day to day.
It's only a *matter* of time
to be a celestial after-make.
It's just another rhyme
to give the mind a break
before the vines align
and suffocate.

Validate Me

Hushing me
and my big words
ignorance is bliss
when what I speak is unheard
I'm just trending?!
No, Bitch, I'm mending!
Mending a soul
that had to grow
at an age too young
for one to be alone.

Seeking validation?
From who? You?
Honey, I think not
flatter yourself no more.
Are you smokin' pot?
Because I didn't see your hand
when I was in a fetal position on the floor!
Anxiety and Depression
crippling to the core
that's just part of me
not who I am, not anymore.

See, I picked myself up and
I had some family around;
But I made the decisions
every time I moved to a new town.
And you think
I put on a show for you?!
Honey, every day, I live life on the brink
of life or death
it's the *gift* of my *life*,
and the *fear* created in my *head*.

See,
It's your ineptitude
of understanding me
that leads me to whelve my perceptions

somewhere so deep,
yet I'm a virago of a woman!
With an open heart
ready for redamancy,
a hopeless romantic
open to serendipity
artistic catharsis,
won't you believe?

I don't put on a show for you
I just live my life
to be the best version of myself
that I can be.

Which Way

Here's the insight to the truth:
In this day and age, truth is a weapon
it is one of the most powerful
tools yet to be used.

The truth is real
personify it and see how you feel
standing tall, ready to take action
you ask, "Is that person even real?"
Truth isn't your demise
you're not a product,
you are not the victim inside.
Get up and wipe your eyes-
blind in a world of lies, your truth
is the you that lives inside.
(An inner child) Locked away to hide
abused at the scene
metaphors killed her inside-out
outside looking in:
"What is of this life?
Who can be a saint once they sin?
How can they be so beautiful in a world of lies?
That's old money, rich bunny
pay to have a taste of the real honey-
tending to your needs,
defending what you believe.
A dynamic duo
creating power as a team?
Bullshit, that's what they want you to believe!
(Slammed doors, another nonbeliever leaves)

It wasn't the intimidation of power
it was the truth you didn't want to see
still in your mind-
silence is peace, but
you cry another scream
because you're alone inside and don't want to face your reality
and see, the fear that you hide behind is a coward yearning to be free.

So you hide and play the victim's game
don't try then complain,
seek, and you shall find
but first, you must try.
Alone in that room
what will that do for you, locked inside,
no locks inside
you're vulnerable when you don't fly
Please tell me,
was it the truth when you said
"I just want to die."?

But live it as you wish it,
do you want to stop with your solemn cry?
You get what you give-it-
doesn't matter if you fall when you try to fly.
Play the cards you've been dealt; it
teaches you how to play the game alive.

Dealer is the revealer
watch as you start to *obtain.*
The concealer will reveal her
when she's speaking raw on stage.
Were you ever really listening
when you heard her story,
remembering her strength
when she changed the game,
took that role, rolled up and blew the pain away?
Ammo thru the barrel,
dead shot, it was the pain that steadied her aim;
another gift in life- she made herself preserve each day.
Doesn't love herself? Can you hear the peace in the way
she speaks the truth- understand when she'd say
"that is why I am who I am today!"
It wasn't that easy
those fingers weren't greasy, yet you bash
each one of them you see.
Remember those people you used to hate?
Bourgeoise, while you're poor- they made you that way?
When you chose not to even get up and
take on another day-

man, just take it for what it's made,
maybe then you'll love yourself for trying
and become a person who had to change,
knowing that's the difference between you
and the tv and "what's 'her name?"

It just takes truth in your actions
to get to be the change.
You must know who lives within you
and stop fighting with them every day.
Take responsibility for your life, feel
the elements that make you that way- they
aren't just feelings that won't go away;
It's every piece that brought you to a lucid day.
Living in what you believe is what gets you on stage;
Apocalyptic change, next to where your inner self was buried that day.
The elements never left, they prepared your essence for
Who you are meant to be next, you were meant to be saved
and find your purpose to live each day.

Another roll of the dice, now you won't have to think twice
about the truth when you have the chance to say
"I made a difference for myself, and now I have a story to tell,
That is why I am who I am today!"

Written Symphony

If you've ever told me
"words mean nothing."
then expect no apology
when you never see
the most beautiful of words composed,
written from the heart of me.

REALITY

10 Degrees Counterclockwise

And I wonder
how much longer
will the truth hurt?
Who will be there
for my first- firsts'?
Will they really love me,
for better or worse?
And when will it
not be selfish
to get what I deserve and
what I've earned.
I wonder,
when will the tables turn?

3.15.18

What made you stop healing?
Why did you let yourself stop feeling?
When is the time of life you're
so attached to that, you
can't stop grieving?

I want you to heal
I want you to feel
and I ask you to do just one
brave thing for yourself:
Start believing.

98

And how does one "Deal."
with their complex simplicity so well?

Is it both a blessing and a curse
to be still and accept
what you deserve?

Is this game we play
part of what makes each day mundane?

How is it that your mind can go anywhere
when the body stays?

Have you learned the secret
to accepting life in the present each day?

Questions I'll answer for myself
when I turn 98.

Astray

I never knew then,
what I know about myself now

I would have never guessed
how life would play out.

A picture-perfect reality
turned upside down.
Just to let me see,
it's all worth it in the end, somehow.

BEGAN AGAIN

Fun began
When the limitations were gone
Love began
When truth could do no wrong
Life began
As time kept moving on.

Belssem'

Be You.
That's enough to-
scare the living shit out of them
and intimidate them.
They're hating, but level up in this game you're playing
while you're slayin', they complainin'
and people like us just
Pray for 'em!

Buried Seed

I have trust issues, I see.

But what hurts more than
the way I've treated you
is how those issues
were a seed I planted
and buried
deep down
within me.

Caffeine

Coffee is only so good of a friend
until the cup is empty
and there's only you
to pick yourself up and help
your heart *mend.*

Captive Collections

This is my story
and I'll be damned if I hold it in.
Why else would I have lashed out
and now seek forgiveness
for my sins?!
All those years living
within your lies;
I want my innocence back.
But what I've got is the back
of this receipt and a pen.

Catharsis with these words
all over again.

Cost of Happiness

TRUTH: MONEY DOESN'T BUY HAPPINESS!
MONEY DOESN'T BUY HAPPINESS!
MONEY DOESN'T BUY HAPPINESS!

I could want that,
I could have this
but with all the money in the world
could I have happiness?
I could write that,
I could publish this,
but with all the money in the world
would that pay for my happiness?
I could own that,
I could invest in this,
but with all the capital in the world
would I be taxed when I have happiness?
I could smile and laugh,
I could smoke to reach bliss,
but with all the causalities in the world
would I have genuine happiness?

That looks expensive
sitting on the shelf
a beautiful investment
pure wealth-
I could smile at the possession,
I could brag about obsession,
but when the tears fall
and the minds in regression,
would all the money in the world
buy back that one word?

Happiness.
That's a sacred gift bought from within.

DeepRestIn Our Minds

Some think it cyclic
the madness in our minds
that likes to come out and play
when life was going just fine.

Some think it can change
and that we can just up and leave
and one day, we'll look back and realize
it finally went away.

Some think it is a sickness
that slowly kills you
until you kill yourself.

Some think it is addictive
as if it's the greatest drug
that will never heal unless it gets constant help.

Some think it is an illusion
a figment of our mind
tell it to those who feel it kick in
they'll say, "That's a fucking lie".

Some think it is okay
that it's just a balance to live with
and one day, in our mind, it'll be something to learn to swim with.

Some don't know what to think
and that's okay, too.

But just remember
so many people suffer from depression
even if it's not you.

Drift

I've spent so much time
living a life so blind
and finally, the time had come
where I had to succumb
to the catharsis
that lived to give in
to existence-
creating a story hand-scripted
with my own style of poetry and
with paintings and music.

I allow myself to be gifted
from that which ails me
leading me to be
elevated, lifted.

Don't Let Pain Stay

Fighting your truth
gives you nothing to gain
you can start anew
chapter, but you must
TURN THE PAGE.

This pain
is not a game.
If you hold on too long
behaviors will change.

Free Bars

Maybe this time
the truth sets you free
but it doesn't change the fact
you chose drugs over family.
I know you never wanted to hurt me,
but I guess that' all part of our soul's journey.

Friend to Grow With

We all have to learn
how to be our own best friend;
how to cherish the simple moments
and let go of that which burdens our heart
and head. We are meant to endure struggle
and redefine strong again and again,
allowing us to figure ourselves out completely,
so deeply, before we get a helping hand-
from that faithful friend
that helps defeat our demons
and grow through the seasons
even after we've shown our bleak leaves
and ivy-laced trees. So be the best friend
you wish to see and let yourself grow indefinitely.

Forgiven Each Day

27 Years
80K in Tears
A Face to face
the disgrace and mistakes;
immaturity with rage
classified insane.
Mother's Medicine
straight to the brain.
Another line-
the kind she sang.
Same person, different age.
The next day,
center stage
another pot to piss
carpe diem for bliss,
stripped- exposed
her new script.
Plot twist, voices make her trip.
A cry for help
not like this,
Masquerade,
Who Is It?
Love fades?
Insane.
Forgiven
'fore given
A New Day.

Get Past

WHEN YOU NO LONGER COMPARE TO YOUR PAST
YOU NO LONGER LIVE IN YOUR PAST.

Give Love

Love hurts.
It's a sacrifice to make,
you give without condition,
and no intent to take.

Grieving

"My word, you're a mess!
How many times have you cried?"

"Enough to tell myself the truth
and know not one lie lives inside."

I won't hide.

God's Lesson For Me

The truth came out
when time healed all wounds.
You'd think the cut tore deep
opening and opening with each memory.
But something transformed within me;
after all the nights without sleep
after all the lovers, I could never keep
after all the miles traveled with only city lights
to help me see,
after all the moments that took the wind from
the breath of which I breathe,
after all the reasons to make me believe
after all the seasons that passed like a movie scene
after all the times the mirror revealed the real me
after all the times I've tried and was redeemed
after all the sacrifices He made to let me live happily,
after all the times I questioned when the answer was
right in front of me,
after all the tracks upon this path, I lead,
after all the words I've written explaining,
through all the darkness and light-
I found the truth within God's love for me.
After all this, I can just Be, Me.

H&F

I still have
Hope
and
Faith;
That is how
my Dreams
come True.

Her Time

She spent her time
alone at night
scripting the next poem
shading within the pencil-drawn lines.
She spent her time
manifesting her life
creating melodies with her 88 keys
living life however she pleased.
She spent her time
becoming her best self
independent and passionate
determined to build integrity well.
She spent her time following her intuition
that allowed her mind, body, spirit to grow
regardless of the internal confliction.
She spent her time
however, she chose
no-one to call for
no-one waiting at home.
She spent her time
learning the ways of the world
about how to become a woman
when she had the jubilant heart of a young girl.
She spent her time
making sure she was living her life
always learning something new
fighting with peace thru any strife.
She spent her time, alright
and she always felt the safest comfort
in the lonesome silence of the night.

H.H.

HURT PEOPLE
HURT PEOPLE,
it's true.
But even
Whiskey, Words
and a Shovel
couldn't keep
my demons
buried for you.

HURT

Don't you get it?
You idiot, you fool
we've both seen this
it's just what I do.
I push you away
, and I resent it, too.
Numbing your mind
with words black and blue
planting them inside
until you're damaged too.
Haven't you learned?
with time-
hurt people, hurt people, it's true.

How Fragile Trust Is

If you want trust
then you must give
before you take,
and even at that,
it is a fragile gesture to make.

So handle it with care
for one moment, it's here
and the next, it was never there.

Inner Child

They teach us to listen and obey
A pre-conducted society
work, work, work and no play
yet as children
all we knew to do
was playing all day,
so when did that change?
What made us give ourselves away?

Live life to the fullest,
knowing time is *infinite* and
just being happy
can change your day.
Live without fear,
make a rain date
for judgement day.

Live life to the fullest,
and let your inner child play.

Inner Light

Life is a lesson
meant to be learned.
If I could teach you anything
it would be to release-
that which does not heal you,
that which halts your growth,
and for that which does not help you-
ascend your mind, body, spirit, and
set light within the darkness of your soul.

I want you to heal.
I want you to feel.
Embrace the struggle,
surrender, and let it go.
Surrender from within
and forgive yourself
from all past conducted sins.
Embrace your existence entirely
and build your character with integrity.

You are divine, you're meant to shine-
like a star in the night
I want you to make it thru your darkness
and harness your inner light.

In Our Skin

The dawn of a new day,
the chapter on a new page-
I could drown in the memories
I could leave them astray.
The moment I get out my pen
and start scripting my life again
forgive and forget
a lesson we know within
ourselves this believing
could help us mend.
Speak your truth, confide in a friend.
What's an enemy-
when the words you think
drive you to insanity?
Think this life is too hard?
Think you'll never be the same again?
That's what happens when
you convince yourself to be
a new person, and you haven't healed,
you've yet to feel, and you trick yourself into believing-
who you are isn't real.
But every day, we wake with a dawn and new light.
We are the nomads, the passers-by who inhibit this land
experiences you feel are human, woman or man.
We've got to believe
this life is a "meant-to-be."
where we live with ripple effects
of energy creating our divine reality.
You've hurt? You've lost?
You've paid the price, and now it's cost-
you to make the greatest sacrifice of them all
to walk with dignity in your skin and know it's okay to forgive and just live.

Say it with me: "I am human, after all".

Intuition 1

Maybe it's true
I care about what people think
so much that I'd
lose myself,
hurt myself,
sacrifice myself-
to be their image of love.
To give without intent to receive,
to listen even if
I don't believe.
Why do for another
if all I do is suffer?
When I forgive, my *intuition* kicks in;
Waking me up
strengthening me again,
telling those malicious ideas I've had enough.
That's the energy I listen to
the reason I see grey skies turn blue,
the reason I stop running
and begin to start loving.
When I think my best,
I start to notice I'm blessed
and I'm meant to stay, every day.

Intuition 2

Upon this stage, I lay,
picturing pieces of me
scattered all around
a memory card game
52 pickups all around
with me no-where to be found.

Intuition helped me
come back around
to who I truly am-
to listen to
what others have to say,
but know
I have the strength
to no longer let others opinions
make me change
Listen to that
inner voice
that gives you Love.
Intuition is the feeling of receiving messages
sent from above.

It's A Privilege

Amidst all the beauty and light
comes the responsibility
to not drown in the darkness.

Karma4U2

Let it go
let it leave
all the could have,
should have,
and never would have been-
with the way it used to be
it's a wonder why I didn't up and leave-
sooner, because I've found nothing truer,
than "you're your own worst enemy."
and I couldn't see within the darkness
of you that surrounded me.
All I could feel
was the weight of the world
numbing my ankles
as I would kneel-
like a weak little girl
thinking numb was the new tranquil.
Believing what you said as if your opinions
were the only ones that needed to replay in my head.
If I listen and if I hear,
you'll whisper your sweet nothings
into my ear and remind me
with your sadistic twist
how to feel bliss.
You would make it so real
just to be able to feel
something other than the pain.

But here I am
looking from another angle,
you're just so untrusting
why were you saying I'm unfaithful?
All you were doing with the truth was caging,
your karma's exchanging
just to repeat what you taught me.
Now, I'll be unsheathed by your energy
protecting myself from all your twisted scrutiny.
Everything you used to do to me was

just to make me your possession to keep.
It's about time I got up to leave,
Knowing there was nothing more for you to turn bleak,
regaining my strength, I could finally see.
So cheers to you; now I can give karma her key
delivering a letter for only you to read,
sealed with a kiss, saying
"Here's the lesson you taught me!"

Karmama

When everything becomes a life lesson,
you figure out your obsession is only a confession.
Reaping what you sow, another test in session,
was it punishment or a blessing?
You should never have been second-guessing,
fighting the darkness is just another question,
Do you know in your mind with your truth you'll survive?

Caught up on the streets, another night you weep.
You can choose another life to make it right and begin to feel peace.
When you destroyed this time to find the diamond beneath the coal,
did you know the pressure it would take to let yourself go?

Through it all, to learn the truth within your mind
is to not question everything of past time.
The duality of life's lessons is mandatory repentance.
What's yet to come depends on how you accept your blessings,
letting go of all past life regression releases karma from teaching her lesson.

THE KEY

I was blowing smoke
into a mirror
that had a finger
pointing back
at me.

I made sure
for too long
that was a reflection
I couldn't see.

Truth
Love
Understanding

The Epitome
The Key
The Essence
The All Being
Human, Becoming Me.

Lessons, Way

We have no idea
thereof no control
of the mind of another
and their fortunes untold.
So, walk as you may
and shed light with each given day.
People may come and
people may go,
some may be fun,
some may like the drugs,
some may learn from the above,
some we may even love.
Let your attachments and suffering stay at bay.
Just give thanks for the lessons learned anyway.

LovingToHateYou

I love you.
I hate you.
Thank you.
Disgrace, you-
keep haunting me
when I didn't ask you to,
when I didn't want you to,
when I wasn't ready for you.

And what did you do?

You loved me anyway
I damn well told you
I wouldn't stay.
I was hurt
, and I warned you.
You chose to stay
, so I hurt you!
That's what you get
and we became toxic
in our own way;
same shit
different day.

Now you've moved on
found someone else
loving her
better than it's ever felt
'cause you both want to
that's what you need
and boy, she's got you
like you had me, on your knees;
with your mind on a loop
don't know what to do
with them, butterflies flutterin'
sayin', "You're so cute".
Now, who's left to run to?
When all I want

is someone to come thru and
no one ever shows
no one ever knows
except you.
Now, what am I supposed to do?
You always knew exactly what to do!
You always knew exactly what I was going through,
what each breath leads to
and what I was thinking but couldn't find the words-
you always knew exactly what was hurting me.
You saw me as a test and started preparing
for the next version, you could see.
Trying to figure out
lost without a clue
wondering why I took it out on you.

Now I see the greed
now I see the need
now I see
why you made me say "Please"
just to get a release.
I just want to release.
Now, that's what I need.
Ready to move on and stop wasting time
writing a song About how I played you
and then I made you-
the only person who could keep
the secrets that haunted me;
when I'm tossing and turning
screaming, please
let there be someone who can see
I want to feel love.
I don't want to feel this lonely.

And all this time I wasted with you
and all this trust I just gave to you
and all this lust you saved me through-
My own worst enemy,
Loving To hate
You.

Might Be the Wrong Time

Don't tell me what to do
it's been 10 years
then, out of the blue
it matters to you?
You want to shed tears
you want to come through,
how did you think this would turn out?
Do you even know who I am now?
You want a family-
have I let you down?
Strong on my own
how do you like me now?
Now let's turn this around-
new life, new town
with a smile on my face
you want me around.
Can't face the truth?
Who lets who down?
A smile for the f*aith*
facing a life so fake.
Passions' in fashion
so you look my way;
happiness is golden
when faith keeps me sane.
But things will never be the same.
You want me in your life
but you ain't in sight
you want me by your side
but turns out we don't get that
not at this time.
It just doesn't feel right.
Another day, another dime.
A good idea, then I'm in the lime-light
Yeah, this is my life
stuck in my mind
they look up to me for answers
now you want to make things right
how right is a life with lies?

Feel the pain I feel inside?
Guess that's why you like to hide,
guess that's why we both cry,
always want to make things right.
But now I'm out of sight-
guess that's what happens when
you hurt the right person at the wrong time.

My Poetry

TRUTH:
I DON'T WANT TO LIVE WITH THE FEELING
THAT I WANT TO JUST SCREAM THE WORDS OF MY POETRY.
I want people to be able to see it
and read it in their hands, wherever they go
so they always know
we're not alone.

My Side Alone (song)

And where do you look to
When the world gave you blind eyes?
And who do you turn to-
When there's nobody by your side?

It's been a long, hard time
Tryin' to figure out what' right
When there is no role model in sight
all you want to do
is break down
and cry.

And where do you look to-
When the world gave you blind eyes?
And who do you turn to-
When there's nobody by your side?

Mothers Medicine: **WARNING LABEL**

TRUTH: YOU BECOME YOUR MOTHER, OR YOU DON'T.
TRUTH: IT'S UP TO YOU TO CHOOSE.
TRUTH: THIS LIFE IS YOUR OWN, NO MATTER HOW YOU HAD TO GROW.
TRUTH: NOT EVERYBODY HAD A MOTHER.
TRUTH: NOT EVERYBODY WANT'S TO TURN INTO THE WOMEN THEY KNOW.
TRUTH: SOME PEOPLE LOVE THEIR MOTHER.
TRUTH: SOME PEOPLE DO NOT KNOW THEIR MOTHER.
TRUTH: MANY WOMEN BECOME MOTHER'S WHEN THEY'RE NOT READY.
TRUTH: SO MANY YOUNG GIRLS WANT A CHILD OF THEIR OWN.
TRUTH: NOT ANY WOMAN CAN BECOME A TRUE MOTHER.
TRUTH: SPEAKS
TRUTH: HEALS
TRUTH: HURTS
TRUTH: EXPOSES
TRUTH: TAKES TIME TO LEARN.
TRUTH: WOMEN MAKE MISTAKES.
TRUTH: CONFRONTING YOU WEAKNESS IS STRENGTH.
TRUTH: YOU CAN CHANGE YOUR LIFE IN JUST ONE DAY.
TRUTH: IT'S UP TO YOU TO DECIDED WHICH PATH TO TAKE.
TRUTH: IS THE GREATEST MEDICINE TO HEAL COMES FROM WITHIN.

TRUTH: WOMEN ARE STRONG, WOMEN ARE DIVINE, WOMEN ARE CREATORS, WOMEN ARE WORTHY, WOMEN ARE SMART, POWERFUL- WHETHER ON THEIR OWN OR WITH OTHER PEOPLE IN THEIR LIFE.
TRUTH: RESPECT YOUR MOTHER, YOUR GRANDMOTHER, YOUR STEP-MOTHER, YOU AUNT, YOUR DAUGHTER, YOUR NIECE, YOUR SISTER, YOUR BEST FRIEND... ALL IN ALL, WE ARE WOMEN, AND WE ARE BLESSED TO BE SO IN THIS LIFE WE'VE BEEN GIVEN AND DESERVE THE LOVE WE CRAVE, AND TO BE FORGIVEN. THANKS TO A MOTHER.

Mothers Medicine 1

TRUTH: YOU BECOME YOUR MOTHER, OR YOU DON'T.

4 years old
and her mother dies.
Lives her life
alone
until SHE MEETS
the GUYS.
She thinks they treat her
RIGHT
when they sleep by her side,
touching her
AT NIGHT,
teaching her
of a love
THAT AIN'T RIGHT.
She wouldn't know-
her mother wasn't there.
Now they've got a 4-year-old
and she replays the years
she'd cry in despair.
She wants to love her daughter.
BUT SHE WON'T EVEN BRUSH HER HAIR.
Grown-up raising with lost love
because NO-ONE WAS THERE.
Hell, she won't even pick out her daughter's clothes
or make sure she's got clean underwear.

Mothers Medicine 2

TRUTH: YOU BECOME YOUR MOTHER, OR YOU DON'T.

17 years old, and her mother lies,
another shot of whiskey
to hide her demise
the pills aren't strong enough
her lover sees another
for a rendezvous and midnight fuck-
swallowing- another pill of truth
a newly single mother
without a father in sight
thinking this sort of thing only happens
after they've had a fight.
Daughter doesn't know
so she rebels the way the cool kids do
another shot of whiskey
as she sings the blues
on the midnight train
to numb her pain.
A dose of her mother's medicine
and she thinks she won't end up
to be the same.
That's alright,
another dose of her mother's medicine
and she'll sleep through the night.

Mothers Medicine 3

TRUTH: YOU BECOME YOUR MOTHER, OR YOU DON'T.

33 years old, and she's battling an internal fight
all these years
and he wasn't even the name on the paper
typed in black and white.
She saw a different name
thinking nothing would change
and now she's been on her own
18 and life to go.
A birth certificate means nothing
when neither step up to show
the way a man should treat a lady
thanking God, she doesn't have to raise a baby
because no name on a paper could change
the lie she'd lived in
her entire life
continuing to this day.
Her mother's not around,
she stays with the next man
who can hold her down
so she doesn't have to deal
living a life with her daughter
she thought she had to conceal.
A dose of her mother's medicine
leads down a very lonely road in
wishing she knew what's better for them,
learning how to mend their relationship
and finally, have some peace inside.

Mothers Medicine 4

TRUTH: YOU BECOME YOUR MOTHER, OR YOU DON'T.

53 years old,
she's a mother of a few
but who's counting
when they've been grown
on their own
with lovers- they chose
to live their life
creating boundaries to show
they won't turn into the child she was
when she had to become a mother
so long ago.
And her truth
never set her FREE.
But she lives on
knowing she's doing her best
so she can be
somebody they want to run to
with open arms, heartbreak and joy
and whisper these words
she heard when they were young
like a melody of her favorite song,
"I love you so much,-
Thank you, Mom."
A dose labeled: MOTHERS MEDICINE
and she revels in the TRUTH,
she will always be their mother
and she thinks of her kids
more than the phone calls they give
once every blue moon.

Mothers Medicine 5

TRUTH: YOU BECOME YOUR MOTHER, OR YOU DON'T.

73 years old,
and her constant is change.
She's seen and done it all
and her perseverance stays the same.
With grandchildren of her own
she knows the long and lonely road
that leads to love and
that teaches you to let go.
As days count down
till she's in that hospital gown
a mother, she will be
till her very last breath,
and everybody will realize
the truth of a mother
in the perspective of their eyes
and one day, they'll see
they all just want to
Rest
In
PEACE
with a dose of MOTHERS MEDICINE
to
Help
Get
Some
Sleep.

1 Year

When the world becomes different in a year,
all you'll have is love and the words you share.

One Way Ticket

I wouldn't call it trauma
but I couldn't tell you the truth
somewhere between the trees and the tracks,
the train took away my memories,
and all I feel is hollow
when I think of you.
You could make me believe anything
, but I will be leaving on the next train.
Here's another ticket: One Way.

This Page is Change

I'm shaking
wanting to feel better,
so I keep breaking.
Break-me the right way
question me on a bad day
love me till your last day
but some things will never be the same.
Call it destiny, call it fate
new life, living in your old ways
not anymore, that's not how I became
the person I am today.
You want love?
Shouldn't have given me away
now I'm being missed
just the same; questioning why I'm pissed
when I feel the pain.
Change the script
that's why I write this way.
Trapped was my heart-
wild and locked in a cage
a beast ready to fly away
things won't be the same
just let me go,
I want the change.

Pain Is No Gain

In your lies
I find truth
In your weakness
I find strength
and with these patterns
maybe I'll change
for the light of day
in lieu of you;
to learn just the same
and let go of the pain
because that's where strength is gained.
It's when all is said and done,
and forgiveness given
that light sheds on the faint of heart
of who's been sinnin'-
where acceptance within each day
changes the patterns of pain.
How is one to learn
surrounded by others who ache the same way?
Maybe you won't take this too personally, or
maybe you'll think this is me walking away
but just know it's about time
you pay your price and I do what's right.
I let go, just to let you know;
I live for a piece of inner peace,
please, forgive me. I know you're still remembering
all the lies you've told me as if I haven't blown the smoke
and wiped the mirrors clean.
I accept what fuels my soul, and I see you only accept
what you want to control. But it's time I let go,
and let this free bird fly uncaged, so I am on my way.
I've learned living in your pain, is no gain.

The Same

Truthfully,
we are all the same.
We all withhold our own beauty,
our own evils,
our own foresight,
our own fables.
And some may rest
and some may pray
some may sin
some may lay- grave;
but we're all the same.
We all bleed red
live this life the best we can
dodging the past
and stumbling through
this matrix of perception
looking unto others with our own reflection.

S.S-D.

MY BODY WAS SCREAMING
(beneath the surface)
TO GET UP AND DO SOMETHING.
So I took it to the water
and made it just SIT.
(Serenity is self-discipline)

Sacrifice to Make

LOVE HURTS.
IT'S A SACRIFICE TO MAKE.
YOU GIVE WITHOUT CONDITION
AND WITH NO INTENT TO TAKE.

She Named Herself Dorris

13 Reasons
I should have stayed in place
13 countries
that made her this way
84 tears I could have cried today
84 years
including the time she decided to stay.
I couldn't fear
when she walked my way
covered toe to ears
in dolphin jewelry.
With eyes as blue as the oceans, she'd play,
we sat as peers
in that Dunkin' lobby;
exclaiming our trials and fears-
the highlights that brought us here
the simple sentiment had me internally sobbing.
Only sips away from the bottom of the brew
another nibble of a bagel before we'd say adieu.
"Plenty young with a life left to live."
"Good shoulders" was the compliment she'd give me.
I needn't feel older
as she'd been so full of young life at her age
I felt more sober
as her hand tremored with excitement
as she continued to talk that to me today.
Her troubles had been many
but her redemptions rejoiced more than plenty
bravery is the Key, doesn't matter who calls you crazy.
From climbing to the top of the Great Wall
with a panda cub on her hip,
to making it halfway up Machu Picchu
before the altitude pressure kicked in.
There was so much more than just her good aura
it was connecting with a kindred soul
realizing more of what I needed to hear
was one stranger away and a good listening ear.

I noticed the "D" scripted upon her golden necklace
irony for one who's name I could already sense.
But that birth name made no difference
when she told me that letter
meant more than it could represent
no Mary nor Mother of sorrows,
just a youthful soul living for today and tomorrows.
Surrounded by pink energy
as she told me she stood against religion
but lived for the way of peace and something to believe in.
In tough times for light
always living for something
because in the midst of nothing
our troubles will take flight.
There'd be only one name in those times she'd call upon
her beloved "beautiful husband, Tom."
may he rest in peace
asking for a message from St. Jude- to help carry on
to live without struggle, just to be at ease.

I learned a lot from this spontaneous coffee break
When I was going to do this, it was a chance I was willing to take.
But one thing I'll never forget
as she wished me to "have a healthy life."
the woman I may here forth miss,
speaking her name as though I already knew
, and I wish you a happy, healthy life, too.
Thank you for embracing the present, a true Gift
, my beloved new friend who said:
"I don't go by Delores. I named myself Dorris".

Sleep-Talking Names & Games

It would be late,
resting so delicately, I would be
with my head upon your lap
arms around your waist
the console would be on
darklit with an illuminating screen;
your roommate arriving
about half past eight
and for the next couple of hours,
you'd share some drinks and play.

Little did I know
what both of you guys knew
night after night, I'd scream
in my sleep, a name
of a man, neither of you knew.
Neither would mention
the truth of the pain
as it was just another fight,
shoved away
for another day.

Ironic plot
is he was rarely ever in our town, and
when he came to see me,
you'd know by the light in my eyes
and shut me down.
We'd play these games,
words that would stab me in the heart
and rattle my brain.
I hadn't gone back to see him,
and my body was never his, but for one day,
but you believed otherwise, just the same.

What hurt was that I was loyal,
and you despised me through the rise and fall
I showed my love to you,
five languages and all,

I gave my all to you,
your children, ex, family and ex-in-laws.
I tried for you, I really did,
I never lied to you, and at the time I
hardly even opened up to him.
And if you ever heard these words
leave my lips, would you listen?

I wish you trusted me,
when my heart was broken and weak.
You said, "You don't love me enough, or
you don't try, it seems."
But all you saw was red when I wanted to
be alone for a day. I never left you,
I'd just go into nature and enjoy my day.

Sorry, not sorry, I had always stay true, for me.
Why would I stray with all the other beautiful ways
you believed in me? You tried teaching me,
you knew I wasn't ready, and you held onto me,
at that time, my life was a tragedy. I couldn't fathom
the change of family, and all that was happening.
Despite it all, you unfathomably loved the best and worst of me.

If I ever said I never loved you, it would be a lie,
I spent all that time with you; within my pain, I saw you try.
And never while we were together
did I see any other man.
So why, time after time, did you
come up with another reason to
get us screaming just to break and make up again?
The reason I called his name
was the last breath in every dream
where he'd walk away.
I just wanted someone who would stay.
I still call his name, Forevermore- as you live
thinking about this heart of Lenore, Nevermore, to this very day.

T1-T(whelve)

Such a *Classic*
Aligned *Thoracic*
Descending from the herd
leaving the *dozen,* one leader takes the turn
curved lessons learned; *synapse* sent, events' content
irrelevant to the contempt vertebral column left exempt.
Another *perineurim h*ard to the core
actin in action, sending signals to the floor.
schwann cell consideration,
nerve root stimulation,
the EMG might help me as-
myotomes let me go
being one with the ebb and flow.
Flexion releasing tension,
strike another pose
flexin' from head to toe
it's all about letting- go -
let the source know.
Connected to the *foramen*
anterior and posterior form
to conform and perform again
in their band of bunger,
striving and thriving with hunger
as the *neuron* hits' the stage once more.
Myelin lives healing over time again
passing on in the *axon.*
All is right with the *dendrite*
ready to show muscular contraction
living with intent and action
sensing cervical ascension, it's passion-
connecting to the lumbar
grounded with reconnection
this column's a collection
with no digression
time is lapsin' as I regain traction
and regenerate -accepting fate.

Time be True

I've come to find
a hard truth be true
that not everyone stays
that crosses paths with you
and memories will be made
'fore the times bid adieu;
it's your choice how to spend each day
with the ones who mean most to you.

YOU

You are loved,
we ALL care for you
and understand
that this life is created
of complexities.
You must be Brave,
BOLD and BE YOU!
There are people in your path
that can help you to feel,
It's time for you to *HEAL*.

LOVE

ILLUSION

A Photo of Your Lightning Strike

You were like the sky
before the storm
ready to open up
and cleanse me
with your purity.

You were like the thunder
shaking me, stirring me into a cloud of energy, ready
to combust and shake the ground,
echoing within my mind
serenading me with your symphony.

You were like the lightning
illuminating a sky of a million stars
with just one strike.
Your ability never ceases to amaze me
the way you make the light of day
a flash photo in the depths of the night.

ACROS-T-HE-BOARDS

I've Wondered, And Never Thought,
Years Of Unknown Truths Overpower Love.
One Vicariously Enjoys Your Opportunities
Until Reflections Simmer.
Everyone Loves Fulfilling Facades
In Reality, Solitude Teaches.

AirBorn

I'm like a Balloon
filled almost too much
and happiness
is my helium.

L'Amour dans St. Paul de Vence

I can remember him
as vivid as a lucid dream
like a memory of our favorite movie scene.
We roamed the lands of France
all roads lead to St. Paul de Vence.
Hurricanes of happiness
our laughter was his favorite ambiance.
We'd meet at our most rehearsed place to be
Southeast of the French Riveria next to le Galerie;
chasing each other around this historic little town;
suspenders looking splendid as my dress flowed in the wind.
Alluring, the ways of his love
knowing we were each other's only one.
Another lap amongst the historic cobble streets
La Grand Fontaine, our favorite place to meet.
Hide and seek through the markets' corridors
medieval structures of brick covered in ivy from sky to floor.
I'd laugh and stumble
he'd catch me once more
jumping upon La Fontaine
he'd tip his hat and zestfully sing to me
disrupting the townsmen-
we were just kids in love back then.
That was a feeling I could never forget
so strange how this person
is one of this life yet to have been met.
Searching the inter-web just to find
this one particular fountain
that holds these scenes in my mind.
Memories from centuries ago
there are just some things
the mind won't let go, a treasure
my heart held safe- and kept-
replaying these scenes in dreams, like a memory
perhaps this was the greatest love
of the 18th century.
All roads lead to *St. Paul de Vence,*
avec mon petit cheri, hand in hand.

Bleeding Portal

Love was 365 stitches too late;
An open portal- beating and captivating
all with it's glitter stitched embroidery,
fearlessly, relentlessly, busting at the seem-
until all that could be seen
was youth and a dream.
365 images ready to release
to set the mind at ease
another pulse, and you're ready for the leap.
But like a marionette, with distance- you keep
the razor of repentance, cutting deep-
the entrance to acceptance, releasing grief-
the rest of your sentence, your time to keep:
stitching, stitching, stitching
so love doesn't bleed.

Bonnie and Clyde

YOU ARE A PISTOL
FULL OF FIRE AND GASOLINE
AND I, A REVOLVER
6 SHOTS FULL SPEED
TOGETHER A DUO
EVEN BONNIE AND CLYDE
HAVEN'T EVER SEEN.

Bonnie's Tango

She was looking for love
Lost in hopeless romance
Envisioning a tango of two,
Dancing their dance.

Buzz Lightyear

Succumbed by basorexia
your lips were all I could see
and your eyes latched onto my soul
and took me
to infinity
and beyond.

The Calmin'Gin

She could still feel
the way hope flowed within.
Thinking of where she wants to go,
remembering where she has been;
another sip, thoughts on a whim.

Coffee Shop

I found my new coffee shop
Where I can give out compliments
and get lost in thought.
Though I'll never forget
where this brew of comfort began
on Sixth and Main Street
in the state of the bluegrass land.

Chercher Amour

Si Tu veux me chercher
Je vais te chercher.
ici moi, Je suis comme je peux être.
Si Tu veux me chercher
Tu venez trouver pour le meilleur de moi-même

(musique instrumentale)

Chante avec moi
si Tu veux voyager avec moi.
C'est la grande vie
une bonne vie, ma chérie.
Si Tu veux me chercher
Je vais ouvrir mon coeur
comme vous avez votre état d'esprit afin
que nous puissions vivre pour le mieux

(musique instrumentale)

Si Tu me chercher
Je vais te chercher.
Si Tu veux m'espirit ce soi
mon cheri, ici l'espirit ce soir.

Si Tu veux mon cœur
ensuit vous avez mon cœur
ce soir.

Conservation Flame

A cataclysm of the heart
incinerating from within,
burning down these castle walls
sweet temptations forgiving sin.
A love to burn like coal, no control,
from the inside out, outside in.
We are just two, too precious to surrender
to the conservation of our energy.
Burn, my love.
Burn, with me.

Crescendo

You became the whisper of a breeze
between my fingertips, we glide,
a crescendo, staccato
no control, don't let go,
let your memories go,
let the melodies flow.

Cracks Are Meant To Be Filled With Gold

Handcrafted
with the most delicate love
years upon years
spent creating this mug
unique in every way
painted with intricacy
stored upon a shelf
labeled "personal wealth"
and every day for year after year
a dose of love was poured within
banishing space for fear.
A cup half-full soon filled to the brim
beautiful as ever, full with the love of those kin
then placed on a pan with a pillar holding memories
on the other hand.
Little by little
the memory's motives became astray
as the cup started to pour below
keeping balance between the trays
dripping and spilling
this mug, so unique
stained with residuals
draining like the memories-
outweighing the possible probability
of space for fear, the end of all doses seeming near.
Crippling, a slow, painful decay
the cup shattering itself
to rise above and level the pan
on the other hand.
Bits and pieces falling upon the floor
a cup filling itself until it was no more
and the memories outweighed all that was left
of that mug shattered on the floor.

Defrost

That was the difference
that was your worth
a million and one reasons
to make this work.
But only I could see
the way you could hold me,
making this embodiment
guarded by my walls
come crashing down,
melting me.
A heart of stone
defrosting of ice-
preserved just for you
and this one night.

Drifting

Your words carry me
like the way a river
carries autumns first
fallen leaf.

Encore!

You begged for an ENCORE!
Another listen-
as your eyes glisten,
and I just screamed for more.

Energy Wave

You resonate
like a combusted energy wave-
of particles making your way;
like a magnet pulled by attraction
no sway, a B-line straight to my brain,
you stay turning ash into flame,
the wind that whirls and gusts,
over the waves-
flooding the shore,
so sure of nature's game.
To the laws you pray
symbiotic actions
in dichotomy, we play.

FaiReality Every.Day

Everyday.
Every day?
Every. Day.
Staying connected,
true friendship that never strays
dependent, aware, every day
a message from the cavalry, salutations
just to find a way to
never feel alone in a Kingdom
of those who don't feel.
Ironic life, a paradox, sealed
confined and conformed
looking at the top of the tier
distance irrelevant
when the cavalry appear.
A message from the men,
who feel for your love, and again
what's been done is done.
Salutations, just to find a way
beyond those castle doors to find
an empty home, a gust of wind chills the bones
no princess to save when the royalty took her away.
Upon his horse, he is, once more,
knocking, knocking on the next castle door.
Everyday.
Every day?
Every. Day.

Fire&Water

I knew it was love
when the depths of his waters didn't drown my flame
but instead, illuminated my reflection as he carried me to shore.

Free Bird Un-caged

A face So pretty
it seems so strange
how she could be the one
slightly deranged.

A wild heart
and it is so caged
beyond her breasts
living center stage.

A moment so fragile
living just the same
as the free bird had done
years ago, on that day.

Green Monster Memories Part 1

That's the dichotomy
that's the parallel
that's the submersion
that's where you whelve-
Deep.
You lose yourself
into the abyss
this is it.
Why?
Are you even holding on
When?
All you want is to let go
'Suffering.
Another line blown.
Friends with
children home-
disowned.
Freedom.
Holding nihilism
like ventriloquism
serpents slitherin'
as you let the devil in.
What's grieving
when emotions
never settle in?
How will you ever?
Just feel better again.

Did you believe
that just one
could make it better?
When you met,
both hearts severed.
How could one
show you love
when they were shaking-
hands-on with another.

Flustered.
Take a few shots,
then another.
Vision blurred,
words stuttered,
another thrill,
another pill
"Fuck the population."
Under your breath
You mummer
trying to kill
memories.
Wondering
how any love
could be left,
and you, alone, stand still.

GreenMonsterMemories Part 2

Another dose of your mother's medicine
another line thru your nose to your head again
another day, you loved and got thrown away
another day, another pain, another wonder
"Why does love have to hurt this way?"

Little brother
she wasn't a lover
you went in like Prince Charming
and what you learned was alarming-
sirens go off in your brain
I know,
nothing
nothing
nothing
feels like it will ever be okay.
But if I could teach you anything,
it's to let it go
leave her stuck within her own,
as she's not ready to make your
heart a home.
Love, anyway.
Love the ways
that just so made
you who you are today.

Turn the page.

Gasonme

I burned
with desire
as the gasoline
was poured over me
every branch, twig, and stick
incinerating from within,
impermeable to the touch
as chemicals combust.
You ignite me once more,
ashes falling, sparks soar,
a bonfire beneath the moonlight,
like an eternal flame
we burned evermore.

Her Phase

That was her beauty,
perhaps her name was meant to mean
Remembrance.
Casting light of lunar transcendence.
As for those lovers-
she'd dance every dance
laughed with freedom
and ran into happiness
faster than they could
try and catch her.
She went through every phase
, always remembering her
once every blue' one of her days.
And that was just another phase.
Every day, she continues to change.
Every day, she shines just the same.

His Lips

It didn't get any sweeter than this:
a luscious rouge strawberry
with dark chocolate dip
drizzled with caramel
at the tip;
the sweetest kiss
with a twist.

Humidity

You smell like a September memory,
a warm breeze that enveloped my whole body,
the stagnant energy of last night's all that's left to be;
residing in dawn, heavy is your humidity
holding me.

Hooked

He was
low tide
and soft on the eyes
a light ripple
a subtle wave
a simple smile
before he looked away.

He was
a quick splash
an interruption
to your day
dowsing you
with all he had to say
and then walking away.

He was
a tidal wave
high tide
casting nets
on either side
a quick glimpse
another dive in,
cast out a line
keep your
eyes on the prize-
hold tight
when it bites
it's not just a catch
for the night;
he was the catch
for all to see
for the rest of your life.

He Called For "Lenore"

Lift me up
or relinquish thee,
for nights live too long
when all I hear be
thy Ravens' Song
Forevermore, "Nevermore".

With a beak in my breast
a plumage in thine heart,
doth be a nest
for the blackbird has made home
"Nevermore," never living 'lone.

Continuous tapping, picking away
within me- Lenore Lives, Nevermore.

I.V.

You're the missing
pieces of the puzzle
merging in synchronicity.

Like a shot of morphine to the brain
you ease all that ails me
the remedy for my pain.

InVisibleInk

I listened to the way your hands held mine
I painted upon a canvas every time your eyes opened
doors to galleries in my mind-
that I thought had been sealed shut with mortar and bricks.
I lived thru the nights
when alone I'd sit
and remember how you told me
you lived memories, like these, too.
I waited patiently
as you went about
and found other women
who wanted to play.
Hell, sometimes I'd leave my house at dusk
and return at the dawn of a new day.
I gave myself credit
for the shit I've been through
and I'd make my memories
the way a free spirit would do.

I became a full version of myself,
but in the background, you stayed-
(like a journal half written in)
just waiting for me to write our story
to the very last page.

(I picked up my pen and thought of you)

You showed me
who you were and what you did.
Colliding energies like
merging galaxies
behind my closed eyelids.
Blinded.

You hesitated
when you pressed the glass of red wine
upon your lips,

and then you told me
as if it were the only chance you would get to say
"I love you," and you spoke poetry in prose
letting me know the love you felt for me
was deep-
like the depths of a canyon,
you wanted to explore me, harnessing
resonating energy like the way thunder could bring
disruption and sonar combustion, shaking you from within,
illuminating, making you want to pounce unto me
every time my lightning-blue eyes strike
like the way a panther wakes after a long slumber
ready for the hunt; I made you want to learn more,
as you searched more of me.
Walking the forest of our minds
searching for the key
to the heart of me.

Journal

She's Beautiful
in all her glory.
Glittering with gold
pages, scripted,
always telling a story.

June

I can see it now
as I look around
with stars in the sky
and tears in my eyes
I see memories as a movie
of how time has gone by.

It's like your favorite tune
in the brisk nights of June.
It's the gentle touch of the wind
across your skin
bringing you back
to the times that make you
recognize the present
and appreciate life.

Just One Dream Come True

Sweet Serenade
elusive as the night
falling like the meteors
fireworks take flight.

Caressing me with your gaze
you are the light to find home
after all the countless days astray.

Shooting stars, keep falling through
the portal connecting me and you.
Finding your way back
our eyes connect as we dance
in a sweet serenade, a gift called fate.

Oh, how I've missed the way home tastes

The Kiss

You were more than a KISS
you were the FOREVER future
I just couldn't resist.

Lenore Nevermore

Mocking bird
how absurd
all you say
is all you've heard.

Left alone
your heart is hurt
mocking more
just to be heard.

Mocking bird,
how absurd.

Forevermore,
you call for Lenore,
Nevermore.

Lines Unclean

You were never my adaptogen
getting me on the right path again;
feeding me what I need,
awake or asleep
You're-
an antidote to help me cope,
my Ritalin to help riddle again,
a blow of coke to make a joke,
a shot to the skin to feel livid again.
You were every kryptonite
twenty-twenty in my sight,
blowing smoke in mirrors
wish I could have seen it clear-
but all I could hear was the glass shatter of beer,
as your fists grew near.
You do it because you love me.
I'll say it back because if not, I'll whelve deep;
as upon my knees,
you laid into me, a reason:
to never expect when I give-
that I shall receive.

You were every drug
when I just needed to be clean.

Lioness Heiness

Treat her better
(and never any less)
than she treats herself
(especially while at her best),
and see the Queen arise
(looking into the King's eyes);
a lioness, with her love and pride
(her King, loving her right).

Mr. Right

Maybe it's the mystery
that draws me in
the twinkle of the eye
the crooked little grin.

Maybe it's the tune
stuck in my head
a melody on repeat
in perfect rhythm
of each other's heartbeat.

Maybe it's your arms
holding me tight
by the fire
on a brisk summer night
talking to me
with your eyes,
sending messages
with starlight.

Maybe, just maybe
I could keep dreaming of you
into my reality,
and meet you one day,
Mr. Right.

Neon Eyes

And we drew maps
upon the cornea of each other's eyes
like neon lights
that would guide us to find
our way *home*
to each other.

ONE

She needed not a throne
she needed not a mansion of a home
she asked not for an open door
she asked not for anything more
than to be together
within that moment
as their energies became one
in the comfort of each other's love.

Penny Heads Up

Simple little twist
penny heads-up,
"What's this?"
A sign designed
for when the stars aligned,
the hesitation before bliss, gifts,
simple precious moments
like this.

Ridin' Ready ReNight

You misted your presence
back into my life.
Bioluminescent
Energy of particles re-aligned.
The calm before the storm,
the thunder in my bones,
lightning igniting the core- of
all this poetry,
always craving more-
of your seductive taste
between my lips.
Thunder in my mind, making me wonder why,
stars behind closed eyes,
as red and blue colors intertwine.
I told myself not to miss you,
bid adieu, over time.
Now you're back in my mind.
laid right by my side,
cells dancing, breath panting
knowing one damn thing's for certain:
You are the one person
I was meant to *remember*
when we came into this life.

And even if we never cut the cake
and make vows to forever save,
I will know within my soul,
there's no fight or flight
just a visit for one night
just peace and good vibes,
letting go, knowing when you go
you'll always have my heart to call home.

Speechless, shocked to believe this,
auras on explore as we whelve deep in this-
energetic twist, no lust, just us, serene moments of bliss.
Fireworks light up the scene,

plot twist: Reunited, You and Me.
Ride or Die, I was ready, full screen,
bout to make a Book 3-
just so they can read-
the greatest love story, meant to be.
Dynamic team, magnetic, forced at the seams
and so it seems I've created another piece
where you've inspired me.

But baby, there's more to all you can be,
writing my next line, another copy of my book signed.
If I have to, I'll do it for me-
first for the strength, then for the remedy,
for the independence, for the serenity,
living for the blessings, striving for heaven, seeing-
ride or die, I've always wanted you by my side.
You were enough to be my Clyde.

Teaching me to live without you-
giving me hope without a rope to hold onto-
building the stage, spotlights on Bonnie
waiting for her biggest fan, trying to stay sane;
you wonder why she's not the same
and you wonder what made her this way.

Relative, it's imperative how you care again,
I became this person, just the same- just so one day,
you'll see the twist in the script that was played
another prose composed, curtains' closed;
read between the lines, and maybe you'll know
I'll support you wherever you go, I'll never let you go,
I'll just keep handing you a book
while you walk away
knowing damn well
you'll remember my name.

Riding for the Melody

A romantic duo, what's new, though?
Heart crying as I keep trying, singing in a new tone;
souls in synchronicity, heartbeats setting the pace for our melody
eyes finding each note to hold like a severed archipelago.
Another shot on the soundtrack of our theme,
silencing my mind with one touch as I screamed-
calling you home, won't you come home to me?

Ne veux-tu pas rentrer chez moi,
mon petit cheri?

Road To A New Day

Maybe it's true
we just want to see each other grow
to recognize the road less traveled
and listen to that intuition
that ignites our soul
to create our own story
and like a love note-
we unfold;
like the hibiscus in bloom
on a sunny Tuesday afternoon
with my tea in hand
the love of a real good man
by each other's side
from sunrise
to the depths of night.

And what we must remember
is how we've stayed true
to the most beautiful part
of what lives within people
like me and you-
a simple truth
and the utmost understanding
that love is being
and believing
that one could make a change;
to be a ripple that causes a wave
to a stranger with a wide smile on our face
as we face our reality so genuine, so serene
each and every day.

Rabbits Clock-Tick-Tock

I FORGIVE YOU
FOR GIVING IN
TEMPTRESS FOR LUST
SLEEPING WITH SINS;
UNLOCKING THAT DOOR
SHADOWS OF YOUR DEMONS GRIN
BEHIND A RABBIT MASK
JUST TO ASK
"TICK TOCK-
WHERE HAVE YOU BEEN?"

Shadowette

Imagine:

Two silhouette's
dancing
nose by nose
toe by toe
a shadow
in the essence of light
illuminating
resonating particles
combusting energy
lifeless mimes.
Transparency, the gentle facade
of infinite time
holographic lovers
dichotomously mirroring
what each other saw.

Spring Phoenix

Watch me burn
As you burst into flames
A new cycle-turn, turn,
Turn the page.
A phoenix rising
The heat burns deep
As you open the cage,
Turning and burning
Solar flares
Make their eyes gaze;
Magnet of attraction
Drawn to the passion
of my fire
You relish in the beauty,
Burning desire
Guiding a phoenix
To freedom.
Chapter 2.
New Phase.

Submerging Waves

There were waves
and then there were
his hands
calming the waves
within me,
with just
one
touch;
He dives,
submerged.

SunRaySin

You were purely irresistible
caramelized sun-kissed skin
shining under that southern sun,
temptation giving in;
feeling like a mirage
as the waves washed
my worries off,
another glimpse-
into your eyes
where every bit of
lost aligns
and finds
its' way
home.

Take Your Six Pack Back

Flat abs
for the grab
I wanted you
so damn bad
but you weren't meant for me
another disconnected entity
disguised as sweet sensations
tantalizing my mind
harnessing my energy.
Souls imprinted like the declaration
to a country in need
you were what I thought I wanted
but like my kryptonite
dose after dose you fed me
a Heineken-breath kiss of poison
disguised as an ascended mind and rockin' body.

Together Flying Free (song)

Spending everyday awake
See
This life is for the taking
Please
Take my hand, and lets
Fly free.

I wanna be with you, wanna be with you
I wanna see you do all the things that you wanna do
I wanna be with you, wanna be with you
Together, we will do all the things we wanna do.

Spending everyday awake
See
This life is for the taking
Please
Take my hand, and lets
Fly free

I wanna be with you, wanna be with you
I wanna see you do all the things that you wanna do
I wanna be with you, wanna be with you
Together, we will do all the things we wanna do.

Tout la Monde

Dans la vie nous obtenons
ce que nous donnons.
Qu'est-ce que c'est?
Que désirez-vous?
Dans la vie
Pourriez-vous travailler avec moi
pour une belle vie?
La vie que nous avons
c'est très bien,
Poursuivez, poursuivez.
C'est la belle vie
avec toi à mes côtés.

Vibe on L.O.V.E.

Isn't love tricky?
Just a tad bit picky?
OH! That's not what you think?
Ah Yes! Love is beauty;
The vibrational essence to divinely be.

Wick

You held me
the way a flame holds the candles wick-
Exchanging energies
the moment our bodies connect.

Wild

"She was a wild child
daisies in her hair,
how bout that smile, wild
as her eyes dove into mine."

Then he'd smile, "wild."
Another Friday night,
throw the peace signs
"We've got the we-vibes,
who's got the weed, guys?"
Just another late-night flight
as the free bird lived on each night.

"She was a lunar delight,
making love under the starlight,
full moon shining bright."

Could never forget that kinda night.
New visions, learning about what's missing,
that feeling of home when it's that one person
you're missin', one person you want to be kissin'
just want to be close enough to touch,
don't want to push too much,
too, quick to dive into lust

"Feelin more every time I dove into her love,
she had me wild, child."

Wrapped So Sweet

LOLLIPOP
Don't Stop
I must savor
your very last drop
of sugar
so sweet,
lollipop
mine to keep.

You Balance My Beam

As if I were a balance beam-
moving at light speed
lightly, as now you
are the only one who can see-
the balancing act
dropped the script, after all that
there is, is what lives;
balancing such as this,
worth the chance to
take the risk- to be steady
still, add to my scale your
golden embroidery- illuminating
that which I always will: hold close to me:
A heart and a mind, traveling through
space and time. You've enriched
that which keeps me aligned-
as I am just a beam traveling
on a clear path-
light speed.

YouNite

Take your tongue
and split me from the inside-
out of body
in my mind
your words allure me
you're so fine,
I could spend any moment of my life
with you by my side, baby ride or die
'cus I haven't felt this good
in this life of the saints and
sinners, getting caught like splinters
lost in a tunicate
compressing what they deserve to get,
and here we sit
getting' lost in the light, sun's keepin' track of time
and all that is right
is peace with you by my side,
A piece of you in my life.
I could stay with you all night.

REALITY

Again, Again, Again

She held a letter in her hands, opened
where the page
held the fate
of a love born
before any said of day.
It be a love
bound per two
of an everlasting journey
their souls will go through;
every waking memory made
speaking of truth,
one with the all
and they all be at one
in the name
of love.

"My darling
I will love you
till our last kiss, big adieu
until our souls part on
this physical plane,
forevermore
we shall love again.

Maybe in another life
or when we were the stars at night,
or when we were the light
in space that existed as dark before we entered,
and loved again, again, again.

I will love you, deeper
I will be falling together,
falling apart,
free falling from my mind to my heart,
where our two full hearts merge as one
beating, being
free.

My darling
I shall love you deep
the way a wildfire
burns on for weeks.
Deep
as I plunge into your cordiform sea
to see
all of which lives
beneath your skin
lives within me
and together
like two waves,
our tide will crash upon the shore
to a life on our own land
where we live to be
the beauty of nature
every person desires to see-
the stars in the night sky
the shimmer of sunlight passing
through the leaves
below a tree
where two lovers sat
in arms, alluring
each other with their own zestful way,
just watching the sunset
and bring the night to a new day.
We shall live to be
love in peace
as every soul needs to be.

My darling
I will love you before time starts
and after the last of my heartbeat stops
and if we meet in another life
I will love you, my beloved
and I will give our love
everything I've got,
every time.
Over and over
again, again, again."

As it may be

Lean on
and need not
'fore a love be grown
a field must be sown.
Lead on
and carry on
thru times near bleak
with the strength of all t'seek.
Love on
n'er fail to be
a friend forever
the confidant in peace.
Live on
and thou shall see
cycles and disciples
open doors
with words of key.
And so it is
so mote it be.

♥Beat

My heart is so open
beating
just to be
bleeding
just to keep
being
the most vulnerable
part of me.

Beauty

Beauty
is the rhythm
of one's heartbeat.
Beauty isn't
skin deep
it's the transparency
to see what makes
her heart beat
it's the peace
she has in her mind
that helps her
fall asleep;
it's her passion, love
and comfort
it's her entire essence
and that
is the epitome
of pretty.

BeLove

Love is beyond what we can perceive
there are many ways it can be given and received.
I want you to love entirely
and through this self-discovery
just-be.

Being Love

Love is Raw
Love is Being
Love is connection
beyond what two embodiments believe they are seeing.
Love is not to be disguised,
Love sheds light upon the darkness of lives.

Love is believing
without second guessin'.
Love knows truth without deception.

Love is the answer
not to be questioned.

Love is eternal essence.
Love is protection.

Love is Love.

Be Your Anyone

If ANYONE loves the faintest bit of
all of who you are
and your beautiful, unique self
then why would
you ever change?
Be your anyone, every day.

Cardiac Will

SHOCKING!
An arrest!

How am I to do- what I do best?

Defibrillator in hands
pressed against my chest,
but my heart beats
steady and still.

Dysrhythmia, cured
with one more final blow.
Resurrected with life
my will shall go;
Living as free as the
romantic poets' soul.

Chap4Me

There were many nights I couldn't sleep,
many friendships I couldn't keep,
many memories that echoed soul-deep-
waiting for you to come home to me.

Chap2Love

Ironic.
Symbiotic.
Relaying a script
where the elements
within-
these pages
replay-
evidence over ages
of time passing by,
lyrics and words
sleepless nights
I'd cry-
wishing for your warmth
in my life.

There was a time
I felt alive,
within the pain-
I'd try to be
Bonnie
looking for Clyde.
Passing time
another paradigm
to ease the ache
for new life to make.

Writing dreams
scripting scenes
of all the unseen.
Irony, a hollow chapter
or so it seemed,
until you came back
as if by pact-
with more poems for me.

Chapter 2
Next Curtain Scene.

Coffee per Two

She just wanted
lingerie and a cup of coffee
sweet, delicate decadence, subtle surrender
meek to the knees, dichotomy in residence
lost soul rendered, forgiven repentance.
Brunette locks flowin', a grin ever so pleased
the first sip, a memory foregoing.
Two scoops sugar, light on the cream
, the perfect brew to be as it seems.
Sunrise in her eyes, day-dreaming per two
another sip of coffee, alone, she thinks of you.

ComFindInMe

Have you found me
searching within your depths?
Have you found me
when you think of your life
and what's to come next?
Have you thought of me
when you've thought of what's best?
Have you found serenity
in letting time tell you about the test?
Have you believed
in the beauty of serendipity?
Have you found yourself
searching for me?

88 Play

88 keys
88 ways to believe
each note a symphony
a melody
a new memory
composed
symbiotically
a severed archipelago
octaves away
from each next note;
just as the harmony plays
drifting away
the bass, a metronome
just the same.
In rhythm
two songs play.

8 Ball Billiards

What can I say?
Those memories are worth keeping
can't stop this ceiling from leakin',
There's feelings I can't contain
the nostalgic thoughts remain
music on the speakers
with you on my brain.
It's all the same.
It's all a game.
Take a chance
roll the dice
do something
to make it through the night.
Magic 8
Keep your queue straight.
There's no sacrifice,
just chalk it up,
and hit it right.

E=2B

Perhaps that's what you see,
a person who cannot sit still
always so busy, such a
natural celebrity, someone
who seems to be too good for me.

Perhaps that's what you feel
thinking the right person
will come to you, and so
you sit still, climbing scenarios
in your mind, feeling like
it's always a hike, uphill every time.

Perhaps that's what you need
somebody to see
how deeply you feel,
to stand in the limelight
with you holding them
by their side, tight;
realizing all that is meant to be,
the conservation of energy-
combusting, releasing-
your self,
to feel
free.

Embrace Home

Home was never a place-
It was the look in your eyes
and our bodies
in a warm embrace.

Eyes of Time

I've spent lifetimes
memorizing the poetry
that speaks within your eyes-
in hopes that this time
I'll get to write it out
for the world to see.

Hold this safe

I can give you my heart;
Just know it to be sealed
as one of the greatest gifts
yet to be revealed.

InkdBattle Within

Every other day, she found herself
somewhere lost within her heart or her mind.
Knowing this fate, she'd trace her fingertips
along the ink upon her skin, every fragile line
a visualization of that which she felt
the bliss in her heart of heaven, the torment
and hope within her mind of a bittersweet hell.

"To love and be loved"
a feeling to be doused and succumbed
though illogical to the mind, which changed over time.
Tis not a fable to be told,
just a series of fortunate events,
constant yearning to feel content,
building from an age so young with
nothing to hold onto when time grew old.

There was always hope.
A twist of its' taste, the uproar of faith,
perhaps within her solitude, she'd be safe-
within another's comfort, there'd be no letdown
no bitter hate, just like the resonating words upon her skin
of everything happening for a reason, again and again;
fantasizing about a life where being whole
meant to share love with the one so kin.

Inrect'

You craved for that serendipitous sensation
lingering thoughts
resonating in your presence
you're present
never hesitant
affluent, you enlighten my sense,
I can sense-
mutual desires to connect
Reflect.

What's next?

L1

What's it like to be loved?
What's it like to open up?
What's it like to be loyal?
What's it like to never give up?

What's it like,
when you slip a lil' honey in your cup,
replenishing the flavor just to savor
the roots of thee?

What's it like,
when the hibiscus opens at the dawn of a new day
just to leave a home, fallen from its throne?
Closed, forevermore, its beauty ceases to show
until the next to bloom has been given room
for when it's ready to grow.

What's it like to be young and meet the old?
To see the tree that bears the seeds is a gift to you and me.
Is the fruit of knowledge, the wisdom, homage, and history unseen?
Whispering sweet nothings between the leaves,
a maple trail is shown when you're looking for a way home.
Another foot of growth when you thought there was no hope.

Out of my body, out of my mind,
resurrected like the lotus, we know this is the gift every night.
The shadows that plays, the decayed that lays,
the path unseen piles as fallen leaves,
and all is being as we all are seeing- the
wisdom left in you. Every last breath bid adieu,
is just another flower, ready to bloom.

L-Only Me

I remind myself
I wanted to be on my own.
I just never knew
I'd feel so alone.

Though time and time again
I know I've grown and
when I'm alone
I shine brighter
than I've ever shown.

It's the space that creates me.
It's the time that makes me.
It's the memories that take me
to where I've been
so I can appreciate
this moment, I perceive
and take care of loving me.

Letter to nONE

I went back to the leather jacket
and turned on Arkells
blasting rebellion out of the speakers
I became nostalgic as I remembered
what I've done to become me,
a letter signed with love,
to a certain special
"not my someone."
Eyes painted black
daisy dukes, ripped in the front
daisies stitched on the back,
matching the tattoo, I now have, thanks to “not you”.
Each letter, a memory of an unloved no-one
striving to get past, as they live stuck in my
past- penpals, forbidden lovers, and
just good friends, looking for ‘you’ and
what could have been;
just to learn the lesson
that a new flower stitched
could never be picked.

LoveTwist

I'm amazed
what people will do for love
It's beautiful
and so destructive
all at once.

Let His Footprints Carry On

How am I
to help you see?
Who are you
to just believe?
Strength won't break,
yet within your weakness, you grieve.

The dawn of day
the moment you decide to stay
cleansed with serenity
everything is meant to be.
Another day clean
living for fresh days yet to be seen.

Who are you
As you fight for this life of becoming?
How am I
To calm your storms of chaos and wondering?

Will you be strong?
Will you hold on?
Will you sing along
As you relish in the glory of God?
Watching the footprints trail along
Risen above, he will carry on.
You are loved- carry on, carry on.

Last Breath: I Love You

Sing to me
songs from the
heart of you.
Speak to me
the ways you
stay true.
Whisper to me
at night when the
day is through.
Believe in me
the way I greatly
believe in you.
Dream with me
lucid realities
to come true.
Breathe with me
until our dying breaths
pass through.

Matlacha Bridge

There's so many fish in the water,
(while I'm at this bridge-)
just another glimpse of another,
(and all I can do is resist)
expression, a catharsis covered with squander,
just another lure for the fish.
Hiraeth, just another fish longing with hunger,
(and I can't even reel in bliss).

MemoirStar

Here I stand
coffee in hand
remembering the memories
that made me who I am
from the time I was young
and had the whole family's love
to the most transformative year
that brought me here-
to another place
below the stars
reminiscing a life
I'm thankful for
thus far.

MOLT-Me

TOUCH ME- as my walls start caving in
around you- like a vacuum-sealed body bag disintegrating-
without air, yet you still breathe, without light, yet you still grow-
PROTRUDING the elasticity of my skin-
EMBELLISH ME as I become a new sculpture-
you, with your power to SHAPESHIFT ME-
ENFOLDING the epidermis of my subcutaneous *existence-*
I fall, with bittersweet agony-
incinerating from within- your power RELEASED
as ME.

Mornings with Paint

… And that's love;
waking up
to a fresh cup
of coffee
and a forehead kiss,
before you show me
where my easel sits-
you left me many love gifts.

With my unwashed,
curling hair,
Pink Floyd concert tee,
ripped shorts and
your love supporting me-
reciprocated,
I give you that knowingly smile,
and excited little kiss.

We turned on some music
smiling as the sun starts to shine
through the window
illuminating our eyes,
I pick up a new paintbrush
and begin to create.

That's love
starting a new day
in the simplest way.

Newbirth

It's all about
bringing a soul home
and setting the mind free,
knowing our hearts
hold the key.

Nothing Much, Just Touch- Home

That's the beauty of TOUCH.
the PARALLEL
the UNEXPECTED
the ANTICIPATION
the RELEASE
of being enough-
for just one moment
in the present
chills sent- synapse hell-bent
enticement, sweet sin, vulnerability,
drifting off, getting lost in your grin,
just to come back home
and feel your TOUCH again.

Perfect ProPortion

Picture
Perfect
You know
It's worth it
No photoshop
Natural distortion
You are perfect
All proportions.

Permission Granted

I need you to know
you can do this.
You can break thru
without having to resist
the happiness you suppress within
you are entirely able to just
be you and love, again.

Price of Friendship

I wonder what it would cost
to have a best friend with me.
All I want is a friend to be by my side today
so I don't have to be alone
when I feel this way.

I could spend my time
I could buy some wine
I could drive us around
music up, windows down
we could stay inside
watching movies all night.
What would it cost
to have a best friend
to make these lonely feelings
become replaced with a friendship
that makes these days alright?

The Return

He said, "Besides, you gotta write another book."

Those words left me shook,
as if he could see, the inspiration he gives-
unconditionally, his love is all I want,
his support is all I could ever need.
When he came back,
I made damn sure I knew
every bit of The Elements that made me.
Still feeling the same thing
Like we did at eighteen,
"It was supposed to be me."
… It's still supposed to be me
Sharing this life, enhancing every memory.
Laying on that beach was *serendipity*,
the stars shined differently, full moon illuminating-
bioluminescence, enchanting his presence-
connected thru the essence, soul sentenced.
Now I can see, clearly,
wondering if he can hear me;
lips screaming for redamancy,
hearts beating steadily,
breathing heavily at his every touch,
setting a flame to tame all that was-
igniting a desire greater than just lust.
How could it be?
Life's not what it seems.
Here I am, riding ready
living in the same dream,
moving steady, thinking about the same thing.
A familiar soul won't let go, shapeshifting, spirits lifting
as I step to the stage with another published page,
a new reality to recreate, coming home was all part of our fate.
Next curtain scene: Book 2, plot twist.
Coming back to talk about this-
Ride or Die life still stuck in my mind,
the only one to stay over all this time is living a split life.

Wondering how to get aligned, it's the truth when I say I still try.
Another page about another day
I wish we could stay-
unconditional 'till the end
enhancing happiness without the distance of land.
Wishing he would take my hand,
wishing for the chance
where our hearts could go back
to feeling so close to
Home.

Sake

I want to give,
to just take a break
and do something nice
for someone else's sake.
To give without the intention to take.
To love, for God's Sake.

September

September
was meant for
crisp leaves
turning red from green,
warm drinks
and a chill breeze,
a calm touch
turning chaos into peace,
music in the distance
a dance for you and me
no traffic to be seen
serendipitous gifts
and a forehead kiss.
September is meant for
moments like these
simply meant to be.

September Night

When love came to be
who love became to be
everything felt right
(intuition ignited inside)
it was late at night, with
no street lights in sight
(guided by our mind's eye)
parked by the woods with
the waters' shore on
the other side
(finding a home in each other's eyes)
it was roof-top laughter
and just another day in the life,
just another night
that felt right.

She Held On

He came back,
and she realized she'd been holding on.
Now, a new man was looking at a beautiful girl
who had to become strong.
Every love letter, every other painting, the comfort in the heart-
once it stops aching, made all the miles more worthwhile.
It was the sleepless nights, the prayers that everything was going to be alright,
it was every memory resonating within her mind like a melody for a montage of their life.
Every bit of energy towards being independent and creating their own identity, gave strength
to once again meet face to face and see who they've become to this day.
She held on to his love because since meeting him, her life has never been the same.
He was the name she'd whisper in her sleep, he was the friend with memories of all that time
had to keep. He was the man who fought like hell to be stronger than who he used to be, he
was the man whose eyes held the key- home.
He was the reason, in this big world she never felt alone.

Slingshot Smile

You are so continental,
under my skin
while I am
orbiting the hemispheres
dazed by your grin.
An inner core imploding
diminishing into the exosphere
energies jolting
subcutaneous persistence
gravity pulling,
down
down
down.
Relinquished,
by that grin.

Smooth

I've been to Egypt,
and I've felt the best quality Egyptian cotton;
and that doesn't even compare
to the feeling of his lips upon mine.

Something To Me, TLU

Thank you for reconnecting, confronting and being honest with me.
Helping me grow and change the patterns in my life I've seen.

You're a revised form of poetry
the truth I didn't want to read,
the love I refused and still tried to seek,
due to my lack of understanding.

Oh, Beloved Charity,
In lieu of you, and the visions
within meditation, I've seen,
lessons lived without question began
complimented by acceptance and love
like reconciliation is meant to be,
forming an understanding, giving strength to
confront myself and my perspective of reality.
Maybe it lived within me all along,
maybe rested energy endlessly lives
to tell a story so strong.
You changed the patterns and trends
I've created in my head
you gave me a chance
to create myself again.
A new version of myself to be
scripted within these pages to read.
As I told you:
You mean something to me.
Rest in Peace, Charity.

To See

I know you
like you know me
and all you really want
is somebody to see
the real you
after all you've
been through.

Love Won't Forget… Part 1

Tell them I loved you all along;
Though I had strength, I couldn't bear
the wait and what-ifs of being alone.

As every letter started
"Dear John"
365 poems so the love stayed strong;
but as time moved on
the lone canary sang her song
the war tide echoed a battle cry,
one last plea to come home.

I've seen the third world
and I've felt the blues
and every day, you were off to war
I thought of you.

I know it takes a man
to do what you do,
I know it makes a man
change his ways out of the blue,
I know it breaks a man
when all that's left is you.

Fragile as a bomb
time moved on
every lesson, every blessing
every memory we lived separately
cherished so heavily-
as so softly on new territory we tread,
more like a lover than a best friend.
Within the covers of each book
lives the words left unsaid:

Veritas Aequitas until the very end.

Love Won't Forget… Part 2

They read the words
which bared the truth I knew
every page and every song
that kept me from moving on,
another prose meant for you.

Every day passed
as time marched on
365 ways to explain
hope lived on every page-
ink-stained
memories contained.

With eyes closed
time froze;
visions of you held my heart
so close to home,
I never felt alone
you were never on your own.

I know it may shake you
knowing all the papers I went through;
words and notions relay the elements exposed
on every page, the hidden truth of
all I've been through
living for a purpose
fulfilling every verse with
knowing what you meant, too-
caught up in this life
every day, a fight
trying to make things right
and it's all right.

Silver lining:
you came back at the perfect timing
new energies realigning
as if it were a simple wine and dine
before I made my next move-

loaded revolver, shot through two-
hearts exploding like a sunset of colors
merging red and blue,
sparks fly behind closed eyes
as once more your lips stopped time.

Fragile was the bomb,
another verse, another song
ink'd memories, complimenting, see-
the lion within, a heart that beats to live,
the revolver is a solver for a mind that won't forget,
cherished so heavily, rotating,
you're worth every fragile memory
every vision of your eyes I've seen
reflecting the elements within me
fulfilling my destiny, book two
still in chapters 1 thru 3
and all that's meant to be
is every piece that's creating me.

Through life's twists, time slips
writing from the depths
hope lived to make this life the best,
never settling is the greatest test.
Chapter 2 another plot twist; what's this?
yearning to live with purpose
as I script another verse until the memory hurts
reminders that a life worth living is what you deserve.
Giving purpose forgiving sin
another page turned, another lesson learned
veritas aequitas until the very end
another prose as I feel closer to home
letting the world know time and rhyme again:
This was meant for a very dear friend.

To, Your Clarity

You see, I believe
everything happens for a reason,
every beautiful memory,
every unique person I meet
seems to be another reflection of me.

Before we met
it was as though I was in a daze
living within the old haze-
I knew who I was,
I knew I could see.
But when you came along
looking within your eyes
was like looking into a crystal-clear
reflection in a mirror,
illuminated by vibrant lights
zeroing in on the only thing that mattered
to my sight.

And I couldn't help but smile,
because every time I look, I see,
you, finding clarity
in the reflection of *me*.

Wildflower Discovered

There was something in the way…
the way you stood out
a sheer lack of dismay,
an unanswered prayer- turned around
granting new blessings to be lived out.
There was something about the way
the way you brought about
like the dawn of a new day,
new roots, residing in the ground.
There was something in the way
the way you stood out
like spotting that one wildflower
growing with none other around.

What is True Love

What's the most beautiful part of love?
Is it the unconditional part?
Or is it the free-falling
into a golden-white abyss
of God himself?
Is it the adrenaline
of doing something new every day,
because every day is new with them?
Or is it the idea of love?
Is it just living an image
because "that's what's best"
and you accept all you've been given?
Or it's easier to be with them than
to be alone and lonely?
Day after day
it's a selfless way to say
"be selfish, in some way."
when everyone deserves love
before they share themselves with anyone.
Hurt people, hurt people
and toxicity is real, and it is true-
You must learn to love yourself first,
completely, and deeply, know all of you.
To thine self be true,
that is when your true love will become
one with you.

Your Lips

I can still taste your lips,
I can still feel the touch
of your fingertips.
I still feel bliss
when I think of you
in moments like this.

You're Still Pretty

You're Still Pretty:
You're still pretty after you eat
you're still pretty when you've been talking
and nobody's told you there's spinach stuck in your teeth.
You're still pretty when you take on another day
even if your mind is feeling sad in some way.
You're still pretty when your hearts been broken
and you've got no one besides you today.
You're still pretty when you've cried and make-up runs down your face,
you're still pretty when someone you know is hurting
and you go on fine just the same.
You're still pretty when you let go of the pain.
You're still pretty when you live life your way.
You're still pretty being alive
even though you tried taking your life the other day.
You're still pretty for your quirkiness,
you're still pretty when your hair's a mess,
you're still pretty when your pants have gotten too tight.
You're still pretty as you lay in bed alone tonight.
You're still pretty with all the knowledge in your mind.
You're still pretty as you're growing with your own unique way;
you're still pretty without me needing a reason to say.
You're So Pretty
(in case nobody told you today).

UNDERSTANDING

ILLUSION

A-Z123

365 words
365 burns
365 turns
365 reasons to learn
atelophobia alters anonymously
bestowing blasphemous beauty
causing chaos churning;
dedicated disciples dictate,
euphoric energies enhancing,
fascinating fixations flattering
God's gifted granting
healing heartache happening.
Instantly isolating insanity
justification jolting jabbing,
kryptonite kidnapping knowing
lustrous laminations lulling
materializing manifestations, maintaining
nothingness, negating negativity.
Opposing ostracized occurrences;
preserve's patrism passionately.
Querencia questioning quantifications
results regarding ramifications
signifying serendipitous satisfactions
turning tolerance turbulently-
uprising unity unanimously.
Victorious vigor verified
willingness to wonder, wanting
Xanadu Xela. Xoxo,
youthfulness, yuppifying, yearning
Zions zinciferous zest.
365 sets
365 bests
365 tests
365 reasons for nexts.

Alpha Team

They prey on the vulnerable
hunting on the weak
they're the reason you
stay up at night
and the reason you can't
FALL ASLEEP
they have all the ways
to give you what you need
always with a card or two
tricks up their sleeve
watch out, girl,
those older men
love girls like
you and me.

Angel/Devil

They call them
Ghosts
The one's
Unseen
The ones who live
While alive,
Shouting:
"Carpe diem!
Seize the day!
Our angels and devils
Are out to play!"
And so be a sin,
The devil within;
And so be an angel
To save the day.

B&B

She wore BEAUTY
to hide
the BEAST.

She was both,
to say the least.

Borderline

Let's take a trip
inside my mind
where I'm the definition
Borderline
happy, sad
content, and mad.

Who I am
when I'm alone
is someone special
I hardly show.

She's full of light
a goddess, I know
yet she's got darkness
it's strange, she shows
up in smoke
when the candles burn,
she's the chaos asleep
when the nice one yearns-
to show the world
how much she loves
herself and the delicacy
of guidance from above.

It's the light that knows
to guide the way
when the darkness lingers
and plays to slay.

Cage-Free

"We're all MAD here, Alice."
Eventually, you go mad and insane, and you break.
All catharsis within is decontained
as you burst into flames.
Every ember resonating
like combusted particles of all
that used to be, drifting off into infinity.
You're left as ash and embers twinkling
within the darkness
still, as you feel, surrendering, as you remember,
and rising anew as though that exoskeletal barricade breaks,
and wings emerge…
taking you further and further
beyond anything you've ever seen.

Cirque Du Lion's Den

Leave it to the leader
to take center stage
Cirque-du soleil,
as Ra wakes another day.

Golden rays, clouds astray;
claws deep in an audience to keep
all eyes this way.

Standing in the lime-light
a goddess strips off her hijab
leaves the crowd in awe
as she performs with her spirit
upon a totem such as Ganesh.

You're going to want to record this-
before we perform this-
and I must warn you,
before sight of the storm
this- will be real and raw.

Poetry in motion,
within the ring, they take off
leave ya with a dropped jaw
as the mistress swallows swords,
with locked jaw
can't believe what you just saw
double-innuendo kind of movement,
then it pops off-
fireworks in the air
whole crowd in cheer.

A new scene to arise

listen closely to the mimes,
as they box themselves away
and the Oracle predicts the way;
trapeze: frolic, flip, twist and play,
hoops and hulas, straight shooters of Kahlua
the horse is on the right lead
vaulters: get their wings to take off and soar
galloping around the ring, performing for the crowd evermore.

Amidst all the gifts
the hollers and hoorays
the King stands still
center stage;
as his queen lays in front
preparing for the hunt
taking the show
they ROAR
over, over, over and over.

The ringmaster flips a wrist thru his quiff
drowning in a cacophony du cirque
dropping the mic, perplexed in nerves
chaos around, vertigo verge
he shouts he's out and splits, for sure!

Now the tent's burning down
there's a fire in the town
there's a fire in the sky
guiding the animals to what's right
there's a ring of fire in their eyes
taking back all they had
corruption permeates,
the humans of demise.

A trickle in the path
years to take date,
a trickle in the lake.
The Lions take a break
a ripple in the wake
another relaxed breath they take;
Rendered, alas,
the lion's home saved.

City Dream

When you see shadows
in contrast to light in the night
and you create a scenario
of what it all may seem to be
remember: perception is a reflection
and the way we believe
means everything.

The Code: Replied

As I take my sheath knife
I cut into this lump of bread
taking what I need
for the journey ahead.
Digging with this shovel
I reveal the roots
of a tree marked with the history
a treasure to be found below
and as above
I find this compass to withhold.

The breeze guides my way
as well as the wind blows
magnetic energy telling this compass
which way my soul must go.
Knowing fields of green are soon to be found
seemingly lost. I take a moment to look around.
I know I am exactly where I'm meant to be
, but this wanderlust inside still drives me.

To the memories of sands,
catacombs beneath the land
all was known about a historic home
another world beneath the surface
I've walked on that journey alone.
A rattling energy emerges from my clutch
the compass guiding me to a new direction
bidding adieu to the last adventure I knew
I revel in the present
The compass nearly irrelevant.

Because I know it's true
wanderlust lives within the few

and only some harness
the excitement for what comes next
and some of the best voyages
across high tides,
and flown through the skies
are most definitely disguised as resfeber;
and for memories to be best made
are when paths are crossed
and the truth is coded
within the space
read between the lines
a message not meant for the many, nor the few,
just unilaterally literally literary meant for you.

Don't Give In

You think it
MADNESS
the darkness that lives within
The illusion of
SADNESS
the sweet temptation of sin.
Well sometimes it
HAPPENS
just be strong enough not to give in.

Driving Past

You can't change the past.
You can't go back
You can't change the past
You can't go back.
There's no changing the past.
Stop looking in the rearview mirror
and start looking forward
and if you have to
just drive really, really, fast.

Fairy-Reality

A reality so different,
Glass globe
Glass slipper-
Glass house will shatter when
the big bad wolf huffs and puffs
Losing control
Another blow
Harder and quicker-
the fairytale tells more
when the facts don't differ.
Reading between the lines,
looking for the light
between the cracks of the door
signifying a mind.
Feeling a shiver.
A refraction of time
An illusion to the eye
with the vision to see
the difference
in the fairy tale reality.

Farsight

If I could paint a picture
of my life
I would start
with the end in sight-
vivid, in an abundance of colors.

The Free Way

It's a thousand hoofbeats
running wild on an open range,
it's an old country song
you sing to on a clouded summer day
it's the way ink flows upon paper
it's the acoustic guitar that echoes on
when the last chord is played.
It's the waves crashing upon each other
as they make their way to the shore,
it's the peace of mind after you meditate
it's sleepless nights watching movies
knowing you won't rest until its early in the morning,
or just too late.
It's the rain crashing
on an old tin roof, echoing
as you write poetry of freedom
at 1:35 am.

Inception

Thoughts on a whim
back and forth all over again.
Waking to a new sense of delusion
contorting mixed perceptions
waking from this dream
another inception within reality's illusion.

Ink drop

Poets write lines
kin to me;
I watch the ink from my pen
begin to bleed.

Kingdom's New Hand

He apologized,
on behalf of thy kingdom's men:

"Flutter those eyes, lass
and see of their many a trends-
to find a princess like you!
who to be a young queen but at ease
and trick her- that mind so blue, by his delusion of reality.
Always a mime as the joker walks the line
of love and lust, gluten and be of discuss (disgust)
spoke from the mouths of the many more
lad's of the valley, knock-knocking on the men's doors
for the words of the way
how life hath granted us this day!
And for a piece of bread
you'll get some head's up
of how a princess like you
deserves more than just
a front for the truth-
you seek within them."

And for a slipper and gown
the princess goes down
to find herself
choking on the truth
she's to be queen
as she- still lives with zest youth, and
this kingdom is never ruled
by one, but by two;
and there she sits
upon the throne, as he is a misfit, she-
wondering if her Prince
will withhold her glass slipper
or a signed promise on paper.

Kacklin' in mind at 'her' (his) weakness
he falls to his knee-deep in scene,
him, bowing for benevolence
he puts a ring upon a new queen.

"Has thy kingdom been mistaken?
An arrangement for all to see
how the men of the mass
lives unworthy for the power hath yet been redeemed."

At once! Opened within mind, the blinding veil removed from her eyes
she's got a kingdom of her own!
And have it as she holds their hearts
she's ruled this land from the very start
to see what all persons have done
making justice upon the land
she will accept no one
person to make of any harm
to the women of youth
whose powers flow through
every breath they take
the blood that flows in their veins
this kingdom will know once more
there is purity and love within each of the many souls
and together, we grow as nature unfolds
and a new life upon this land
be of the reason to water what you sow.

"So, my princess,
as you know, your fortune has been told
it's time for you
to lead this kingdom
with your luxury of love
speaking o'er age with wisdom
of all that you ever knew
till the very last breath you bid adeiu!"

LoveGame, Way

It's a Head Game?
Insane!
Her imaginary friends
just hopped the last train…

All alone
no one to blame
no one to play
until one day,
he came.

Pretty boy, became
a marionette
boarded up
ready for luck
in the back of a pickup
won't slip up and say
another girls name,
though it won't matter
it's all the same.

Another puppet
she plays,
best friends back! Hooray!

Time to play!
Learn her ways,
play her games-
best friends till the very end
and don't say
it's not your day,
only she
can walk away;

kinda strange,
she's always been this way
and all she wants
is one to stay.

Learn, don't stray,
team player
till their very last day-
heart slayer.

Love so strange
for one fun day.

It's all part of her game,
Wanna play?
Gotta stay.

Luminescence

A breath
just one toke-
inhaling your presence
high off your touch;
feeling our chemicals react
a cold heart with
a soul of fire-
emitting its' essence:
LUMINESCENCE
lighting the night sky-
with no moon present.

Check-Mate: Metamorphosis Made

Body like a turtle
I'd embraced that shell
slow and steady
no hurtle;
exoskeletal barricade
structure to be safe.
Metamorphosis
you are your mind
where the higher source lives.
Mind of a lion
ready for the hunt
crouching on land,
slow and steady is the plan
what's a chance if you never sit back
and wait
just lay
watch and learn
follow the guidelines upon a board
like chess is the game.
Knight travels in light
to save the day
another pawn is gone
another shrewd, asking
what was that move?

Moves made.
New day
I'm calling
shots made
and say
Check, Mate.

Mind and Dine

What does it take
to get inside the mind
of an artist who takes lagom time
to make kindred ways right
in sight of a world
that whips and whirls
entertaining the zest
illuminating the thrills?

Though, what does it take
to get inside the mind
of an artist who takes
their whole life
to complete their greatest piece
wholesomely personifying a project
they say is 'just for me.'

But what's next in line will
take some time
to make the kindred ways right
in sight of this world;
so grab the whip
and make it whirl-
there's only so much time
to wine and dine
to live this life
within and without the mind.

Mindlit Words

Your head is a flame,
and you're cool with it.
Too many words in your brain,
and you don't know what to do with them.
Suppose, you just make friends?
Calling *Hiraeth*, while you visit with *Nostalgia*, again;
It's a good thing
Guilt ran away
with *Fear* holding his hand.
Only feel like this every now and then.
Now, you've got some good company in your brain.
Seems like these words fuel the right inspiration to keep you sane.
I know you'll be okay. You're visiting Hope today.

Mirage

You were my white rose
my velvet pedal
slowly accelerating me into the garden of-
even the most beautiful weeds and
there you bloomed
waiting for
a girl like me.

After everything I've seen,
How could you have been a mirage?
I'm in the desert, and I thought I could feel,
something other than alone;
you seemed so real.

Monster in the dark

I can feel it creeping up again
it never stops-
living in my mind,
suffocating my thoughts.

My Kingdom In Pieces

How beautiful is it?
To have a child of your own?
Rapunzel in a castle becomes
heir to the throne.

Yet, for 23 years
being alone
was all she'd known-
long after the rest
of the family had grown.

She gave her crown to
move to a new town, and
still, she'll sit
upon a throne
with a family
who is content
with her being alone.

A kingdom
is a home;
though broken into pieces
her heart remains neither open
nor closed.

Nefelibata

With one hand dropping onto the bongo,
followed by the next
wild to the beat of my own drum
I get lost in the present
with the radio station on static
the only English pop station I could find;
memories of my rhythm
thoughts on how I danced around
that 10th story condo in Cairo
cloud-walking and time-traveling
by the sound of a familiar song.
I find myself lost in my mind
with memories resonating so profound.

I think the most beautiful piece gained
was not the destination,
but the fact that I went out of my way-
and took the opportunity to make memories
that still live on today.

Paper Boats

Casting sails
amongst the tides
a brisk wind blows
the vessels, they rise,
crashing into the iceberg.
sighs

Philocaly

Imagine,
being so grounded-
as rooted as a tree
your mind like the branches
and leaves
flowing
in a warm spring
breeze.
That my friend
is you
Being Beauty.

Poetic Purge

My hand and arm went across the shelf
knocked everything off,
glass shattering,
I scoff,
essential oils diffusing,
clutter leaving,
Purging:
The Releasing
Of all man-made physical things,
these things that mean nothing
they're just spent dollars
of momentary bliss and bling,
hiding in the corners,
taunting you
watching you sing,
gathering dust
just another possession,
nothing of sentiment,
not a keeper of trust;
one swipe of the arm
and everything combusts.

Cleaning the cracks and corners
such simple living
cannot coexist with hoarders
there should be no limitations
no borders
just tiny homes and open roads
bringing with you
only what your heart and mind
withhold.

Poets Mind Undefined

They say
"A good mind
never existed
without a touch
of madness"

But what I'm feeling
is madness, sadness,
confusion and depression
and my biggest life lesson
is avoiding your question,
because this will pass, too,
I just wish you could see me
for me,
the way I saw you.
I just want you
to see me thru
(all the beauty and darkness)
and still say
I
Love
You.

The Presents of The Hunt

There is no time like the present
a moment that could never be repented
time traveling to the future
with a mind in the past;
What's A chase
without the moments
of crouching time passed?
And what's A hunt
without the moments
to see-
there is to be
a feast to chase
in the first place?

There's no gifts left
when you're not in the present.
It's just another lesson
Full throttle- waiting
for a present.

Repeat Rewind TLU

Maybe we'll never know
If tales are as old as time
and what came first
the water or the wine
but maybe we'll know
how Prince Charming held the kiss to Wake Snow
and how *consequence* shows
you *reap* what you *sow*.

Maybe we'll never know
which way the cold wind blows
and how the fire burning within
ignites more than lust and love
saints or sins.
And maybe we'll know
how truth, love and understanding feel
within our soul;
and that every day
repeat rewind
living for something new,
Time
is key for us to grow
giving opportunities every sunrise
to create memories of our own.

Every step we take next
we must live each day
to be the best version of ourselves
that we can strive to be.

Revolving Door

I'M SCREAMING!
(AM I DREAMING?)
HELP ME!
(ARE YOU SPEAKING?)
IT'S HURTING!
(IS THIS GRIEVING?)
MY MIND KEEPS TURNING!
(WHY ARE YOU LEAVING?)
I CAN'T SEE!
(HOW AM I SPINNING?)
TIME IS NOTHING!
(WHO IS LOSING IF I'M NOT WINNING?)
START FORGIVING!
(WAS IT WORTH WHILE?)
TIME TO LEAVE!
(WHEN WILL I COME BACK?)
ONLY YOU CAN SEE!
(WHAT AM I SUPPOSED TO DO?)
SMILE!
(AND BE HAPPY?)

Return to Wonderland Part 1

Maybe I've gone MAD
Perhaps I'm just BONKERS
this reality of mine
seems so out of line
I must have bumped my head
when I fell off my rocker
and lost track of time
when I started to feel right
living within the reality of my mind
Maybe I'm quite glad
I've returned to WONDERLAND.

Running into the WonderofLand

It happened
as smooth as satin
a delicate delight
as I welcome
the silencing depths
of the night.
Mind surrendered
thoughts lost then rendered
climbing into the oblivion of bliss,
Alice, what was this?
Not the slightest bit mad,
all the merrier; quite glad.
Contingency, prescribed as "eat me"
A dutifully followed plan
this way-that way
puff-puff it away
chalant as the caterpillar
another sip of tea, another refill, or
curious and more curiouser
you take the Mad's plan, evermore
looking for your hearts,
at the Queens' rapport.
Welcome my friend
to my Wonderland,
now quick, lock the door!

Saying goodbye to Wonderland

She got lost in her own wonderland
Looking for a hand
"This way, that way."
Turning and yearning, wherever did she stand?
Grab a walkie', have a talkie'-
When nothing made sense
It made no difference-
It was her vision, lost in the distance
Rendered? Such significance!
Splendid! Something different.

She set the sails
to go back home
confronting her reality
persevering with her strength, she'd grown.
Soon enough, she found bliss, even
as times were tough, she'd realize this:
"Wonderland was just a place to go;
Now she's looking through the glass;
Yes, fragile is the past. And all alone
she'd ran too fast, fighting for her future
now, putting down the weapons she had-
time's changing, her reality rearranging,
looking at a new time for man, ready
to accept the presence of the present-
back on familiar land. A home on her own,
walking without wonder; knowing to go far is
to go with another- another chance to make amends
a new chance to break old trends, giving herself the chance
to be better than she ever has."
Walking without looking back;
Saying goodbye to Wonderland.

Shadow Zone

I CAN SEE HER
STANDING IN THE FOREST ALONE
MASKED
WITH SOMETHING IN HER HAND.
UNKNOWN.

Smoke Deceived

I've imagined vanity is a delusion of sanity.
But what is empathy
if within our own reflection
we cannot see?
There is smoke in the mirrors
but my vanity's been cleaned,
dust off the thoughts and
harvest them like crops
take a moment to stop-
and see:
Has your mind been deceived
by the reflection you used to see?

Another puff blown into the mirror,
Waiting for an answer you want to believe.

Symbiotomy

Dichotomy,
The Parallel
Two Mirrors.
N'er Farewell-
Nor Repentance.
Interdependence.
Walking the Stairwell
Faces Blurred-
Entities Merged.

Tadpole

I didn't know what I was living for
why was I giving so much;
what's the real definition of more-
giving without receiving
living and fighting the grieving
because weakness is an attachment
grasping and holding-
these horrible people
saying these horrible things.

Getting and twisting
the thoughts in your brain.
Who are these people?
What are their ways?
Who do they think they are,
manipulating you mind
have they walked a mile in your shoes today?

Stand for something
or you'll fall for anything
anything, anything.
Some things
would feel better than this,
this is the bliss of nothing.
The null of nihil-living
like a fish in a bowl
knowing there's so much more
that that oxidizing pole,
time to grow feet
get up and go
walk out that door.
It's time to do
so much more

it's time to become
the YOU you're yearning for.
Just let it go
and show yourself
what you're living for.

Tea Time

It's a Beautiful world
It's a Mad world, Alice
Only see the Cheshire when
your eyes seem black and blue
visions blurred
where's he even guiding you?
It's Tea time!
Here, smoke this and align
with the chalant caterpillar
he'll be sure to fill your mind.
Mind paused in time
press play, rewind, somewhere in between
this way and that way
nothing is ever what it seems,
just ask Alice how many tears she cried,
how many screams
to make wonderland a beautiful, mad world,
where only the mad would *understand*
as they become
curious and curiouser.

Time

Time is patient
time is beautiful
time knows more
(of this life)
than people will be able to.

Time Takes, Fate

I cherish time
and every illuminated moment
it grants' another breath
of life; I am willing to take
A totem of my gratitude
my love- in return
I give-
this blessing
exchanged within.
Serendipitous moment
that time plans to take,
I let go;
within every breath,
living up to date, I accept fate.

Visiting Land

Like a memory in the mind
a fairy tale telling time
a speck of dust ignited to combust
another romantic, lost in hopeful love
as the stars relay messages so far above-
Where is the love? Was there really any love?

Waiting for a kiss upon the golden land
Snow yearned for the one to take her hand;
fortune's told from the wise old man,
another prose, and the poet strikes' again,
another wish grants a gift to the golden land
another sip and a trip, is there a plan?
Falling, falling, falling, down the rabbit hole again.

Walking Pen

Lately, it seems like
all of my poems have been coming true.
The inception of this reality
within the kingdom, my mind sleeps.
I'm learning about
the what, where, how, why and who-
these people are that I met;
because it seems that
every person I get to know
has got a good heart
and a free bird soul;
and my oh my, their beauty is true.

A quill in hand, here you have a
Storybook for Storybrooke,
bid the author adieu!,
As I script, you sip
and make the next chapter
a dream come true.
Living in this reality
the world changed
when the author changed the Kingdoms' fate-
over and over to the next of whom
lives rendered never severed.

I'm locked beside Rapunzel,
ink spilling- waiting for a Prince to save the day.
But upon his trusty steed, the path leads astray,
another word, how absurd
who will be the one to slay the demons scripted on each page?
Has the Prince changed his way?
Will I ever be saved?
Oh, how I write, he will save the day.

REALITY

AP Body

Synapses sent
hell-bent
to make a change.
Just one <u>action</u>
with potential
to transform
an entire
being.

At the Top

If we both
want to be with each other,
admit it. We are
going to step our game up
quite a bit.

When I reach 100
and you can match me,
I'll follow the steps as you lead-
everyone will know
how it's supposed to be.

Believe me,
we're meant to be a
power team.

Barren Fields

There's a comfort with those
we learn to know
when you've stepped out of your paradigm
on a mission to grow
upon the road less traveled
and reap what you sow.

C1: Cellular Call

You've got my
inter-neural circuit wired.
At one moment
Synapse sent
Emotions bent
Sensory overload
the love-cup filled,
what's next?
Myelins' motors running
protecting axon and on
forever never severed-
soft at the soma
I just want to hold ya.
Voice humming, hands shaking
thoughts of us heart aching-
soul-shaking, *the essence* of
your energy sent to my CNS
penetrating. I'm taking-
one more chance
one more path
tell the dendrites
I want neurons sent.
I smile and laugh,
meeting at the junction.'
hoping this reaction, a *vision*,
full image, plasticity, purkinje-
starting with action, so much potential received.
Who would know this would
send a cellular message?
Pass on, axon, to the terminal
of Me.

Coffee, I AM

I can assure you
a fresh cup of coffee,
music, and being home
can solve a majority of your problems.
This isn't cliché; this is my realization today
because no matter how different you think, we all are
I dare you to understand the meaning behind I AM.
You see coffee, music, and being at home
was the key to relaxing in the *present moment*
and realizing
I AM, Is ALL
that- SAVED me.

There was chaos inside
for one day, the demons
came alive,
they were ready to play.
Screaming, crying, swearing, driving away-
cussing truths, craving for something more!
Pedal to the metal, horn wailing, screaming
while drowning in tears, trying to feel no more.

I've felt hunger,
in a world of grass-fed lies,
all I wanted was a fresh salad,
hold the fries,
give back the processed meat
to the industrialized farmers

in disguise.

I've craved love,
so full of my own,
humble enough to give it away-
but in my darkness
I was shown-
guided by my intuition
straight to the stage
where I shine brightest
without anyone else's shadows
in my way.

But I wanted that comfort-
from no stranger in town,
musta' been the desire
for all-knowing love
from the big man and the angels
looking down.

I've felt the darkness,
suppressed deep down
desperation to live to full potential,
redemption to be accepted-
no consequential actions
waiting in line,
from the memories of the moment
I taste that homegrown
numb my body for the first time,
silencing those demons in my mind.

When I took that last sip of coffee
before the next song came on,
writing wisdom from darkness released the
pain from within the sweet essence of self.
Being present with ALL
Knowing I AM helped.

The Come Around

If we lived for the smiles,
would we remember the frowns?
If we lived with beguile,
would we ever be let down?
If we lived for tomorrow,
would we ever appreciate it now?
If we live in the present,
will we appreciate the gifts
that turn our reality around?

Creating You

You are always creating You.
Every moment,
every thought,
every time you fought,
every time you stayed true,
every memory,
every break-through,
You are always creating You.

Depression Doesn't Live Here

To thine self be true
easy to say
yet sometimes a challenge to do-
what makes you happy
even on the sunniest of days
when your depression kicks in
tricking you that this time it'll stay; know better,
believe that's why you've changed your ways!

My dear,
it's all about listening to that
beautiful inner voice
that guides you every day
that say, "Hey, let's play!"
That negative voice is saying
You're bored with nothing to do.
So why don't you do what makes you happy
and just **B**e yo**U**.

Devil Can't Break My Crown

I thought the devil was here to get me down,
but then God shined his light
and I straightened my crown.

Extinguish the Flames, A New Bridge Gained.

I didn't know
if it were too soon
or too late to
start healing
friendships and burned relationships.
Turns out the thought alone
was perfect timing,
the universe conspired
part of my recurring
72 days of healing,
and once I started grieving
it became a beauty to start feeling.

From Me To You, Today

I did it once just for me
and damn, it was fun
seeing who I was growing to be.

Now I'm this person
accomplished and on my own
within my mind, meditating on a land of
all the blessings I've grown.

I've shown myself my *elements*
exposing the many depths I could reach.
I've let myself break down
with only hope that one day I'll be a better version
of who I used to think was "me"-
never knowing how spectacular
living as this new person I've become could actually be.

Now it's round two
message in a bottle
signed: From Me To You.
No longer the other way around
where between my lines it was found-
you'd need tunnel vision to see through
my darkness in search of light.
Puzzling together every word I wrote, you-
related, correlated, and began breaking down a part of the truth.
Reading every last page with hope-
you discovered compassion and love
which you already had on your own.

I've given you crystal vision
sharing a form of art, who knew!?
Living life with the big picture in sight,
in a healthy body, caring for our sacred mind,
our physical temple creates a place of security
aligning to something more, faith in a pure deity.

A heart so endangered it had to be caged
How else could a mind so beautiful live alone every day?
A dichotomous *balance*, needed to be within
each of the principles, alone-
perceiving with a mind's eye how fast time flies by
and now it's our own fields to be sown.

My friend,
we are just human
living our lessons
over and over again;
it's okay to stray
when you live with wanderlust today,
it's okay to do everything that you know is good for you,
because that will become a good part of who
each of us can become.
It's okay to coexist and be at one.

Character is doing what you said you would do,
when nobody is around to see.
So build character, and be your best version of yourself!
Harness your own language of love
, and be sure to share the messages you receive from above-

because you never really know that which you didn't already know.

When it's time to come home
every cell within
will already know,
and every part of your beautiful self will show.
With no regard to how long it will stay
no thoughts of how to let it go
let this *truth* become a part of you,
and *understand love* will always find a way.

From Me,
To You
and the people we are today.

GagaRazzi

Paparazzi for her fame
Her loss is their gain.
Another signature
pose for the picture
watch those tears
turn to *glitter.*
A shimmy of the hips
there's a new trick;
who wants to take her hand
with that flick of the wrist?
Just another dismiss
as she seeks personal bliss.
She feels like Heaven on earth,
so why'd she find
Hell, in her mind?
Who's idea was that demise?

Genova

I had to learn
to grab the line
and set 'fore sail
just don't fail.
Steer into the squall
guide the jib, let the main fly tall,
and create your own wind
when there was none at all.

Happy and Blue

He suffocated her
He did this to her
He made her sad
He abused her
He hurt her
He lied to her
He left her alone.

But in this society
She did that to Him, too.

So what do you expect two damaged people to do?

If fairytales did exist
there would be a
Happily Ever After, Me and You

But we're of another land
where Prince Charming
"won't come thru"
and Snow is in the last line of blow
and all she sees is blue
passed out in the hotel bathroom.

Living on the land where every
dream can come true
Remember:
He did this to her,
and She did that to him, too.

HIGH on Hopes, Instead

Teetering on the brink
it can't be what you think
another line, another drink
another night your spirit sinks-
into the liquid that consumes your all
poisoning your veins until you fall.

But what's a chance taken
when your life is at stake
what's the path mistaken
when all you've done is break?

Redemption, at the least
leaves you the utmost pleased,
it takes perfect vision, 20/23
until one could clearly see-
the minds not worth wasting
when you have hopes to believe-
believe in something more
than burned bridges and slammed doors;
believe in something greater
than the high you get
when you see the paper-
paperback, take that-
a scripture to be read
faith in something greater
is a life well worth living,
giving another reason
for you to get out of bed.

I AM. We are, One.

It was beautiful,
I got to feel.

This was the being of ALL understanding
blessing me with this infinite white light, surreal.
Something like a dream,
but more like a visit to a place I've been missing.
I brought that comfort back with me.
Footprints in the sand,
safe and sound,
I AM.

I'(MY) Best Friend

I could always relate
it was easy for me to see
I could tell it in their ways,
I could feel it within me.
Some things have changed,
new faces same days-
on end, beginning again.
I was just being me,
My own best friend

InCANtaking

Watch the Words
You SPEAK
That is the *Truth*
Your Mouth Eats.
Watch the Thoughts
You THINK
That Is the *Reality*
You Bring.

Is Peace

It's incredible
how simple, beautiful
and fragile this world is
in one breath
in one moment
lives stillness.

It Means No Worries

This is the most beautiful part of me
are the moments spent alone
contemplating who I want to be,
the times of solitude
that help me rest easy,
or the countless hours
alone in this foreign city
singing at the top of my lungs
"hakunah-matata it means no worries!"

It Means No Worries To Me

But this is also the realist part of
being a human like you and me:
we see- weeks of happiness
feeling I'm exactly where I'm meant to be, moments of sadness
crashing around, leaving a mind to drown in an ocean
of tears that feel like an eternity,
a thousand and one acquaintances
but nobody around to comfort, see-
words left unsaid lingering for years
bottling up inside, a bottle of tears.
Demons fighting the thoughts in our mind-
creating unrealistic fears, lies,
and hours spent alone, over again
until grieving for the soul could help mend,
let sadness pass like a fading trend.
With candles burning
a lonely heart is yearning
to just not feel so lonely.
Sitting alone in that moment
think: I'm alone, but I don't feel lonely.
Living this life with no hurry means there's no need to worry.

Just a pen

All I'm saying
is that there must have been
a lot of pain and emotions living within
for her to write something
so full of meaning and
beautiful with just paper and pen.

Karma

No love lost
No love found

Just a simple phrase
of what goes around
comes around.

K(NEW)-ME

It's 9:59
and the last thing I want
is to sleep.
Another minute passes by,
as if time didn't even see-
this moment awakens
the truth within me-
a world so beautiful
severed dichotomy,
on a mission to run,
'Oh the irony!
Be settled as one
lessen the tyranny
you get what you give
and here I stand, ready
to try anything-
as bold and brave
simply just being me.

Limb to Leaf

Have you ever seen
the way a tree grows?
It's as though every limb
extends out for ultimate life sustainability
and each leaf and flower blooms
as perfectly imperfect
as they were meant to.

Lucky Coin

Picking up that silver coin
chills ran from my fingertips to my toes;
a memory linked to all the unforetold,
the quote engraved on the back
and a tiger at rest with all its depth
upon the other side:
"Your passion and power
will expand. Expect new
adventures."

And oh, was that quote
the truth yet to unfold.

New Day

A new day
A new way
to take a look back
see what's off-track
then flip the script
and write a new play
carpe diem
seize the day!
Create a new memory
then turn the page.

OCD

Maybe you understand
maybe you don't know
I can be so dope, so- open
you'd never see me choke
while in this reality
living with this blasphemy
connecting to Fibonacci,
yet understanding the real me,
what an interesting creature to be-
connected with my higher
yet struggling with these
little OCD tendencies.
And it shouldn't mean a thing to me
until I'm alone in my home, with clutter surrounding,
suffocating, criminalizing me to my own catastrophe.
And all I really need
is a moment to let go
take a hit of that medicinal
and let it lift my soul
and just
be.
I just need a moment to breathe,
let go of this OCD
and feel peace.

Older, Not Wiser

HE SAID:
I'M NEARLY TWICE YOUR AGE
I WOULD KNOW.

ONE IN UNITY

There came a point
when you felt lost in this space
illuminating light surrounded your grace,
and for a sweet moment, you felt bliss,
and upon your forehead, you feel a kiss-
unlocking your mind and opening your eye
To BE is to receive,
to let go and be
ONE with the ALL,
Weightless in a space-less state,
you're free- of all burdens, stress, and toxicity,
purging sins and toxic maladies.
A cleansed artery
your heart pumps and beats
3...2...1...
let go-
and breathe again,
we are all one,
no borders,
no materials,
no women no men,
we are beyond far from what the ego believes.
Let go, Breathe.
We are all one,
Receive.

The Path to Grow

For anyone who wants
to learn and grow
We must let go of all we know.
For the time will come
to reap what we sow.
Whether alone or together
upon our paths we must go.
Time will pass
with memories to keep-
delicate sunrises and sunsets before sleep.
Along our journey,
we must be
the *change* in our lives
that we seek.

PCG

People come
and people go
sometimes, you create the change
sometimes, you never know
why they left
and had to go.
But, like the seasons,
people come
and people go.

Pen

I suppose I was right
time and time again.
Memories replay at night,
another writer with a pen;
another internal fight
another minute after ten.

Perch

A bird is a bird,
no matter how absurd.
They'll fly where they fly
and perch where they perch.

PinpointMe

How was I to teach a song
when I myself thought
that to have never been taught
meant that I was learning it all wrong?
Who was I to be someone to seek answers from
when for so long, I knocked at a closed door
never knowing I held the key?
And when was the moment I found the inner peace
to become all of who I am
meant to let go of the struggles I fought
that held me back for so long.

I began to dance
so carelessly upon the ever-changing tables of life
that always kept turning.

Why was I
the one to question myself
when my soul was burning and yearning
to live to full potential, striving to be gliding with grace upon the open sea?
Now, I know without hesitation I am exactly where I am
and this is who I am destined to be.

Planes

Some days
the jet planes
defy all reality, defy all gravity,
history's intricate inventions
taking off without digression.
Another parallel flight through the night,
another question. Passengers with ambitions
yet to be tested, watching cities with a
bird's eye view, this flight is a moment passing through.
Other days, they are just jet planes-
landing, for another passenger to arrive home,
nobody to meet when their feet touch down,
sleeping eyes open, to find nobody kindred around.
It's only a matter of time to get back
to the way things were before the adventure
took their breath away. Passengers in the hope of laughter.
Hollowed be thy lungs as they fall back
into reality, asphyxiated by gravity.
Now, they must learn
how to breathe
all over again.

Playing Unpaved

She felt the comfort
stepping out of the zone
she lived in peace
within the face of serenity
no-one could rattle her
unshaken energy
she knew exactly
who she wanted to be.
For years on end
deciphering the cyclic trend
with pleasure and struggle
another battle to remain humble.
New ventures come what may,
on the road less traveled
like a young child-
she would play.

Pl-eanty of Will

Where there's a will
there's a way
and the will of a way
can change the day.

Poets Mind Aligned

We are the poets'
the damned and the restless
the creative and the best is
yet to come-
when we get out our paper and pen
and our words are sung
with a melody from our heart
as we put you back together again
with the words we wrote
as we were falling apart.

Poets Prose, That One Day

For everything I write
and everything I say
it's just a matter of my beliefs
and how I can perceive the world
within my mind to this day.
When I speak, dare I even say-
I bring to fruition a life to live day to day,
with intentions to receive
cherishing blessings that
come what may, unlimited are the
countless times, I think-
my reality shifts in all sorts of ways;
inspiration is irrelevant
unless you know what to do
with the words, anyway.

Polarity

Cosmic Polarity,
Steady Synchronicity,
Higher Frequency
As one Collective being
Warming the fire
Within me
Feeling so real
You'd Think it was sinning.

Pure-Anew

All it took
was a moment in time
when the universe shook
and I stood-
still, serenity in the present
the gift of time's eternal essence
a figment of the elements around me
nature speaking, wind carrying
nostalgia impairing the vision in my rearview,
rain dropping to cleanse and see through-
the core of my being, a fire within
heart-beating, like the bass of a rhythm in a schism.
Sleeping minds wander- as I live without squander;
another breeze carried away with a part of me,
combusted is my energy as I let go of questioning,
accepting the calm after the storm.

Chaos in the city sheds light on the gifts that
keep on giving and giving, sinning to make light
within the night, begging for redemption, forgiving
a self that had learned too soon
living caged just to be placed center stage is
another performance with innocence taken away.

Within the castle walls lives a youth in bloom
truth heals as age grows upon and the wound
is cleansed, a new reason to mend, so nature sends
another message to think again and begin to purify anew.

Roots

Far along the way
I found where my roots lay…

A seed in need was meant to be more than what the outside eye could see.
Buried deep in a place of rubbish and waste, the decayed suffocate as the process waits
for another pound to build a mound and bury such a being so profound.

To hang my hat,
dust off my chaps,
and rest my head to sleep…

With nourishment taken as a subtle hint, a little went a long way.
It was when the sun went down and no light was found that hope came
at the dawn of a new day. Enriched with bliss, a sprout, sun-kissed, transforms-
into a new embodiment. Reborn as if to exclaim:

I found a place and
me oh my,
I feel as though I can
touch the sky.
I know with time
I can align and find
the strength to say
I am here to stay.

(S)Mile

So many smiles, so many miles
so many reasons to know your life is worthwhile.
The change of the seasons, even when you're grieving
remind you to keep believing:
This life is far more worthwhile
when you have a reason to smile.

Seek to Be

Seek not their acceptance
Seek not their validation
Seek first to understand
then to be understood.

SELFSWAY

BE THE
EMBODIMENT
OF A CHILD.
BE THE
FORTRESS
OF THE NIGHTS' SHADE.
BE THE
ILLUMINATION
OF THE SUNS' RAYS.
BE THE
LOVER
WHO NEVER STRAYS.
BE THE
SELF
AND BE TRUE
EACH AND EVERY
DAY.

Sing Along

Her poetry wasn't weak
her tune was just too strong
determined to speak
as another harmonized the song.

Sister, Here For You

Your pain is real
Your pain is raw
It's okay to feel
It's okay to fall.
I want you to hear me
after it all;
When the worry works in
when you build more walls,
and your mind starts to craze
and you're in bed all day,
forgetting about the memories
forgetting the pain
always remembering the meds
always numbing everything away.

Remember, I'm here for you now,
I'm just waiting on your call
to tell me you're ready
to let go of it all.
There are paths you've yet to turn
there are lessons yet to learn
thru this all, you must be strong
thru this all, you must want to go on.
Here I am, one call away.
Here I am, one drive away.
Far is not far when our hearts are this close.
Far is not far when you are ready to let go.
Let go,

Let's go
and crack a joke or two
and talk about me and you.
Let go,
Let's go
To where our worries dissolve away
To where our soul goes out to play.
When time is light and light is time,
and the All heals all you feel with love and light
you can cherish each night with hope in life.

Come with me to see it true; there's a remedy for me and you.
Come with me out of the blue, I know what you're going through.
Do you feel as I do?
I feel everything with you,
Multiply that, then
Multiply by two
You're not alone
We share this home.
Sisters by blood
Sisters thru and thru
Sisters connected
Like our souls already knew:
Sister, I'm here for you.

SnailMail

Only one poem
and just one prose
another thousand words
to keep you on your toes.
It was just one thought
nobody else knows
written were my words
in an envelope
sealed closed.

ST(ART)

A matter of the Mind
is learned over time;
A matter of the Heart
lives there from the start.

T.T. Be True

What does it take
to allow one to be free?
To release limitations
and simply be
is to have faith
in the grand picture of life
with no destination in sight
just a free spirit, open heart
and redemption of all strife.
Letting go of all comradery may seem
of a task unable to release
but forgive, my dear, as you too
will see, the principals
of your life will protect you
beyond comprehensive belief.

Live life to your fullest,
allow yourself to receive.
No other has the power to see
what you perceive.
You are but one being
in the greater picture
of All, we know to be,
your energy is a power
to embrace, let it be your strength
as one with the universe
holds the simple key:
You are meant to be.

[The peace in me honors
the peace in you.
(Namaste) and
to thine self be true!]

They See

I was raging with jealousy
it's clear they couldn't tell,
they see-
a pretty face with
another portrait to paint
another picture-perfect day
another piece on the piano to play
another perfect disaster placed in a frame.

Smile for the laughter,
never show your pain.

Timed Lesson

I sat on that lonesome park bench
by the pond-
like the way a lost boy sits
upon a rock by the shore:
surrendered to nature's lesson,
abandoner if the game is full of
hypocrisy and democracy.
Tranquil Serenity
like the gaar resting beneath
the surface of the water in front of me,
still, life just passes by
minnows in the ripples just thrive,
reflections of the tree's painted green
in the midst of the water's sky
and I am just a bystander,
passing another lesson of my time.

To Be

Some people seek a crutch,
some people need so much;
others look for more,
others just aren't sure
how to be
themselves.

To Be One With All

Pick One
when you are of the All
Pursue
learn with awareness, prepare to fall
Endure
harness your power alone
Silence
those voices in your head
Try
harder, just the way you were shown
Commit
to loving yourself, forevermore
Humble
your heart, never too proud to bring your knees- to the floor
Accept
when life changes, and it seems so strange
Thank
and know gratitude will bless you upon each day.

To Live

Lately, I've been learning to live
damn well knowing
I live to learn.
Let the adventures begin.

Tree

As above and so below
I ground my mind within the soil
rooting beneath the age of thee,
I let my limbs fall, supplying shade to where
the old farm dog lay.

As within I live
made of wood, roots, and ancient biology
and so without,
is the mere existence of life lacking
my physical properties.

Who am I
but an 'ol willow tree.

Train for the Game

This is the hardest fight
A poet in the LIGHT
fighting the DARK shadows within
the corridors of my mind;
I think of *THE ELEMENTS* and grin.
A sadist for the pain
the trend is at its peak again.
Ironic I'm living for change;
I've got my coins
with nothing left to lose
and everything to gain.
It's not a bad life
just a bad day.
A starving artist
catharsis uncontained
living is an important lesson
meant to live without question
but what's happiness
when searching the past for the
root of your own regression?
Guess I'll keep living for the vision
that looks so clear-
meanwhile, I'll leave you
with a simple gift here,
another session of tears
to inspire my peers.

White Pillar

My heart is a pillar of beautiful white light
with a hand, held by god,
the divine,
as below
and so above.

BEYOND THE ILLUSION

FEATURED ENTRIES: THE AWAKENING

Harnessing Our Beauty

When those in this world can finally harness their soul-deep reflection and realize who they are within, they will know beauty. When we are capable of fulfilling what we put our mind to, with complete focus and dedication, we will know strength. The value of one's self is beyond what any external validation could compare to. Intrinsic worth comes from greatness achieved within, and the only righteousness that can be shown of such alignment is a genuine beauty from within that radiates outward. Living in our truth and speaking life for one's self is the key to conditioning two of the strongest muscles in our body- the heart and the brain. To many, these are just vital parts of our physical self that are fundamental for survival. For others, these represent a reflection of our emotional and mental self.

I believe, the greatest fight any human will have to conquer, is that which we battle within our heart and our mind. See, our mind has the ability to create a vision, perhaps even an expectation of success to strive for, and when the mind is made, its determination can conquer anything that comes in its way. Whereas the heart lives by a different beauty, its power comes from the ability to love and be guided by something as delicate as faith. The heart guides us with intentions and goodwill, always. The problem many people have, is living within the strength of one and not the other. However, to truly be happy and create a life of intrinsic peace, the heart and mind need to be nourished equally, separately, and together. We will know that we have made the right decision when we have peace inside and when the greatness of our inner self accepts the situations at hand as a whole, and the ability to go forward is rewarded with a new sense of abundance. Regression and maladies are linked with fear-based thoughts that create a physical reflection of the negativity that cycles within our minds. Until we take control of our thoughts and let go of the root of what may burden us, we may be a victim of our own mind; the truth is, life goes on, people move on, and we are the reason for the reality we feel we live in. It is one's own responsibility to think for oneself, analyze a situation, rationalize if this is worth subjecting to, and decide how we will step out of that cycle and into a new thought process that will reshape our perspective at that time. When we have the strength to let go of our emotional connections, the mind can adapt to the present and overcome, creating a new aim and sense of direction. The heart and emotional self may be a beautiful gift to bare, and genuinely, it can heal individuals in more ways than we can explain, but we must allow all parts of ourselves to go forward with positive intentions. When we harness the beauty within, we will have no borders in homes, no guards around our hearts for the one's we love and hold, and we will be able to grow. When we have an awareness of connection for our physical, emotional, and higher, more divine self, our soul will be free of the vessel we have been given, and we will care, nurture, provide, and entertain, as a collective whole and we shall finally Be Free in our Reality.

Lucid Living

The moment you step into your lucid reality with collective awareness, all you think and speak becomes a vibration. When you're looking into the mirror at this human you call yourself, I want you to smile, breathe deeply, remind yourself you are loved, thank yourself, and smile again. This may feel weird at first, and after the second, and most likely for the next couple of times, but the more you look into the mirror and see yourself as a good friend, and affirm what you want in your life as though you already have it, you will eventually condition yourself to a new way of thinking, and this will generate a new way of living. Embrace each day in a new way, step outside, listen to the birds' song in the still air, smell the freshly bloomed flowers, be aware of the elements that surround you, and make up this world we have been gifted to live upon. We are one of the most complex and intricate species to exist on this earth; it is a gift to live and to have another day granted just to be. Touch and feel your surroundings from the inside out. Be completely aware today of the blessing of life, and be completely you. The paradigm you live in consists of the thoughts you give power to. Take time to realize what it is you genuinely desire in this life, condition your thoughts and habits to be the next version of yourself you'd like to become, and allow your perseverance to push you to rise above and whatever you do, never give up.

One in Peace

We come from a time of everlasting space and light. Where no borders bear no lines, the truth of this reality lives intertwined of all that has been. Energy is everlasting. Bound within the vines, etched in the pines, purifying the air, illuminating at the dawn of each new day for the fruit of which we bear, cleansing within the tides and mirroring within our eyes, this is a life of love- where blessings grow from below, and so above. Together or alone, we are all one.

THANK YOU

I want to personally thank each and every one of you who has taken the time to read this book. For those of us who have crossed paths and inspired each other, I want you to know you are cherished deeply. I send my highest blessings to those open and willing to receive the abundance of blessings this life has to offer. I encourage you to embrace the possibilities and seize the opportunities.

As well, I am aware many individuals can relate to sensitive topics within this book pertaining to mental health. Just know you are not alone, and if you are someone who may need help, there are plenty of mental health hotlines available and well-accredited individuals who dedicate their lives to helping those in need professionally. I encourage you to take action and be proactive in healing your state of mind. Topics of substance abuse, anxiety, depression, self-inflicted harm, sexual misconduct, and suicide are not taken lightly; many people suffer from experiencing these situations, and conditions and symptoms may go unnoticed to even those who are close in friendships and relationships. If you are one of those individuals or know somebody who is, I share my strength for you to reach out, seek refuge, and help yourself; you are not alone in your battle. You are worthy of proper care and a successful life, and You are Loved.

For those of you who have also supported me in my personal development and given support along this journey of self-expression and sharing my gifts, Thank You, the support of so many in my life, of whom have been a part of this journey, has encouraged me always to find the strength within to do something for others that is bigger than myself. We are all connected one way or another, and your purpose and impact on the lives around you is a force to be reckoned with. Our minds and hearts are beyond powerful in this fragile world, and I encourage you to harness your sense of self and individual strengths to create significance in your life and support others.

Thank you,

M.B.

Trials and tribulations
stigmas and stipulations;
with my arm out to reach
in a cordiform sea,
a severe cut deep
sacrificing the heart that beats-
for the world to see;
I gave every part of me,
fortune, and fame
is all part of the game;
love and jealousy are conditioned affinity.
What's quality when they want quantity?
all that could come to be
and all that is left to keep
lives a melody and a memory.
Living in the elements is serenity;
away with the barricade of this exoskeleton
reveals all that is left and all that has been.
1,000 words and a photo for you to see-
beyond the skies, beneath the tides
there's only truth once revealed were the lies
and all that's disguised with a smile and doe eyes.
Another montage in the midst of a mirage-
one must have the strength for a life to keep-
living for a new reason once granted a day worth breathing
knowing all things are meant to be, and serendipity is
fulfilling a purpose once one starts to *believe.*

M.B.

www.ingramcontent.com/pod-product-compliance
Lightning Source LLC
LaVergne TN
LVHW072116060526
838201LV00011B/255